The
WATERFOWLER'S
BIBLE

The WATERFOWLER'S BIBLE

ERWIN A. BAUER

Revised by ROBERT ELMAN

⚓ **Doubleday**

NEW YORK   LONDON   TORONTO   SYDNEY   AUCKLAND

Published by Doubleday, a division of Bantam Doubleday Dell Publishing Group, Inc., 666 Fifth Avenue, New York, New York 10103.

Doubleday and the portrayal of an anchor with a dolphin are trademarks of Doubleday, a division of Bantam Doubleday Dell Publishing Group, Inc.

Library of Congress Cataloging-in-Publication Data
Bauer, Erwin A.
  The waterfowler's bible / Erwin A. Bauer; revised by Robert Elman.
  p. cm.
  Previous ed. published as: The duck hunter's bible. 1965.
  1. Waterfowl shooting. I. Elman, Robert. II. Bauer, Erwin A.
Duck hunter's bible. III. Title.
SK331.B331989   88-4219
799.2′44—dc19   CIP
ISBN 0-385-24474-6

The 1965 edition of this book was published under the title *The Duck Hunter's Bible*.

CONTENTS

The
WATERFOWLER'S
BIBLE

INTRODUCTION

THE WONDERFUL WORLD OF WATERFOWLING

Late in the afternoon a soft rain began to fall. Before night it would probably turn to sleet and then to snow. But now Bill Browning and I huddled beside a bend of Red Rock Creek and listened to the patter of rain on the old camouflage-patterned sheet of canvas that covered us. I shivered.

"We shouldn't have long to wait now," Bill whispered.

Some might say that only a pair of madmen would waste a late autumn afternoon in Montana beside a brook formed from snows melting in the mountains. But duck hunters would understand because we were *duck hunting*. The evening before, Bill had watched flight after flight of mallards funnel into this place from all around, and he figured they would return. So we were waiting.

While we waited the weather changed from bad to much, much worse. First the rain became sleet and a cold vapor came pouring over the Lima Peaks of the Rockies to the west. The vapor quickly spilled into the valley—Centennial Valley—and enveloped it so thoroughly that we seemed to be suspended in a void. We might have been on another planet, so strange did it seem.

The temperature was dropping. Although I was wearing woolen socks and insulated hip boots, I wiggled my toes to restore circulation. As the sleet began to freeze on the canvas, Bill shifted, adjusted his cap, and turned its flap down over his ears and the back of his neck. That was when the first ducks came.

Eight, maybe nine mallards buzzed in so low they almost skimmed the canvas under which we crouched, and then they braked to a sudden, noisy landing in the creek not thirty feet away. In the next instant they were gabbling softly and nibbling on the green watercress that grew lush along both fringes of the creek. They didn't suspect danger was watching them at close range.

"Now," Bill said.

Together we threw back the canvas and jumped to our feet. For an instant time passed in slow motion; the ducks couldn't believe what they saw and they only looked at the impossible spectacle of two humans on this soggy bank. Then a hen squawked in alarm and Red Rock Creek exploded.

Maybe someone else can explain why only one drake dropped after five shots—three from Bill's pump, two from my double—were fired at relatively easy, flushing targets. But that was the score. We looked at each other sheepishly, laughed, and crawled back under the canvas.

"I hope that wasn't the only flight," Bill said, "or we'll have more of your uninspired stew instead of duck for dinner tonight."

My waterfowling friend needn't have worried, because what followed was a hunter's dream of paradise suddenly come true. Mallards began pouring into that pool as if it were the last place on earth to find open water on which to spend the night. They came as singles and doubles, by the dozens and by long, irregular strings. Before the legal shooting hours ended we had a limit apiece, unloaded the shot-

The world of waterfowlers is rich in scenes like these: the morning's first flight of ducks swinging low over the decoys on a Texas marsh (*Joe Richard*); an Ohio hunter preparing to head home with his limit as the sun goes down; an antique clock that awakens gunners in an old duck club.

Sunset on a waterfowl refuge in Maryland.

guns, and then just watched the remarkable performance until it was too dark to see any longer.

Because of the overcast, the ducks came in low, just above the ground. There seemed to be no end to them. Several times they practically brushed the canvas with their wings. Others just materialized out of nowhere. Some kind of natural radar guided them. This is something, I kept thinking, that should happen to every duck hunter on earth. It was certainly an incident I would never forget.

But to tell the truth, the sport of waterfowling is a *series* of events a hunter will never forget.

The wonderful world of duck hunters is something special and something different. It isn't as grueling and tense as typical big-game hunting or big-game fishing can be. But it has some elements of these plus escape, tradition, suspense, and a tremendous uncertainty.

Duck hunting gives one a chance to see the loneliest places. Nonhunters, who wouldn't understand, might call these the unfriendliest places. I mean blinds washed by a rolling surf, blue and gold autumn marshes, a northern bay with ice forming on the perimeter, a rice field in the rain, flooded pin-oak forests, or any remote river delta. In duck hunting the scene is as important as the shooting; at least it is for me.

The scene might even be completely unreal. My best example recalls an evening in Baja California when Glenn Lau and I were sitting together beneath a thornbush on a narrow finger of gravel beach. The beach separated the salty Sea of Cortés, near Loreto, from a murky green, brackish lagoon.

We were there to collect enough whitewing doves to broil for dinner, but that plan soon changed. Instead of doves, small flights of bluewing teal and black brant kept buzzing into the lagoon. That in itself isn't so unusual, but nearly all of Baja is a sunbaked desert and the waterfowl came bursting in to us out of an incredible desert sunset. It was one weird duck-

Waterfowling can sometimes be hard work. Above, the author crawls on his belly to get within range of cornfield geese. At his side is a honker bagged in this manner when it flew up from a field of stubble. Below, Larry Koller carries home the rewards of such work—a Canada goose and a mallard. Koller was one of the great hunting writers of the 1950s and '60s.

hunting scene never reproduced on calendars or postcards. But we had the kind of shooting nobody ever forgets.

A day in a duck blind can make serious hunters—even addicts—out of otherwise normal outdoorsmen. This is a sport in which, for the best results, you get up long before daybreak and remain out in the elements when they are the worst. There are duck hunters who will disagree, but on the average, shooting is best when the weather is least pleasant.

The influence of duck hunting on men is also evident in the great amount of money spent every year to pursue the sport. Today many of the best waterfowl-hunting areas are leased or owned outright by duck-hunting clubs. Some of these amount to no more than the legal papers which describe the lease or ownership. But others are fairly elaborate clubs and many border on the luxurious.

Depending on how elaborate the establishment, membership in a duck-hunting club can be downright expensive. Besides the club buildings, a number of boats, guides, dogs, decoys, food, and bar supplies are necessary. In many cases there is also the matter of constant maintenance of dikes, channels, and water levels with heavy equipment. Obviously the expense is great.

But so are the rewards. A day in a duck marsh means much to many men and the cost isn't the greatest consequence. An official of an automobile company once told the writer that the ducks he bagged one season cost him $1,238.98 per pound of meat. But it was worth it.

"You see," he explained, "I live ten days a week during duck season."

But not all waterfowling is expensive, as we shall see later on. Some sportsmen with little to spend also live ten days a week during duck season. As in fishing for sophisticated trout, this is a sport that can put a man's ingenuity to great test. If he is a clever hunter and willing at times to labor—even to sweat and to suffer—he can enjoy duck hunting that money alone cannot buy.

Duck hunting has an added fascination because it can become a year-round source of interest and activity. In few other sports is a dog a more valuable ally. And to get the most out of a duck dog—a retriever—is to spend time all through the year in training and conditioning the animal.

One duck hunter who squeezes more out of the sport than anybody I know is my neighbor and foul-weather friend Frank Sayers. I say foul weather because we invariably get bad weather when we go hunting together (which fortunately is often). Anyway, Frank built his own duck boat and decoys during the off-season, annually builds his own blinds, and has trained his own Labrador (from a puppy) to be a first-class duck dog.

You could safely say Frank is the Compleat Waterfowler. I have been with Frank when the shooting was very good and when it was very bad; he has fun in either case. He has also suffered. Several years ago we were jump-shooting on Big Walnut Creek in central Ohio. With us was a big Lab male, Blackie, borrowed from a friend. It was the tag end of the season and most of the creek had frozen over, with only scattered areas around riffles containing open water. In these spots blacks and mallards were concentrated, plus a scattering of goldeneyes.

We made a classic stalk on one riffle and neatly folded up a black duck on the flush. The bird fell in open water and instantly Blackie plunged into the icy water and grabbed the duck. That's when complications began.

Blackie couldn't get back on shore because he couldn't claw his way back onto the ice sheet surrounding the open water. The dog was in bad trouble. But not for too long.

Frank stripped off his pants and boots and without hesitation broke his way through the ice to belly-deep water. There he grabbed the Lab by the loose skin on its neck and dragged him out onto shore. Ice froze on both of them.

When we were finally able to thaw out Frank and the dog with the car heater, Frank's first comment was, "Did you notice that Blackie held onto the duck through the whole thing?"

I had noticed. I had also noticed other good examples of how waterfowling makes addicts of men and their dogs.

But how about the ducks and geese—the targets of this book? Altogether there are 247 different kinds of ducks, geese, and swans living somewhere on the face of the earth. They range in size from the tiny (less than a pound) Indian pygmy goose to the huge magpie goose of Australia and the trumpeter swan of North America. Some ducks verge on extinction, others seem to be prospering. Owing to a recent series of drought years, the populations of some North American species have declined and may take some time to regain former levels. But in southern Argentina and New Zealand professional hunters are employed to shoot geese wholesale because they are a nuisance to agriculture.

Some species of ducks and geese must also be considered among the most beautiful birds in the world. Most American shooters are familiar with our exquisite native wood duck. But the woody has plenty of competition in the good-looks department from such as the mandarin duck and Baikal teal of Asia, the red-crested pochard, and the Siberian red-breasted goose. The last is an aristocrat among all birds.

Some ducks live more in trees than on the water and others are found only in high torrential rivers of the Andes Mountains. Some prefer steaming jungle, while close cousins never leave Arctic barrens. Some are shy and furtive; others, like the Cape Barren goose, may attack anything of any size anytime. The world's waterfowl comprise a highly interesting and exciting family of birds. It's a shame that the future for all of them is not brighter.

Of the 247 world waterfowl, about 44 live in or occasionally visit North America. For the sake of describing them in this book, we will divide them into four groups: large puddle ducks, small puddle ducks, diving and sea ducks, and geese and brant. A separate chapter is devoted to each group.

Puddle ducks are typically birds of fresh, shallow marshes and rivers rather than large lakes and bays. However, this is not a hard-and-fast statement of habitat. They are good divers, but ordinarily feed by dabbling or tipping rather than by completely submerging.

By contrast, diving ducks frequent larger, deeper lakes and rivers and coastal bays and inlets. Nor is this a hard-and-fast statement. The divers are usually grouped together because they do feed most often by submerging, often to considerable depths.

Ten kinds of geese and brant and three kinds of swans may be encountered by American waterfowlers. Two of the swans (the trumpeter and whistler) are native, and the third (the mute swan) from the Old World is now semiwild in places.

Although swans were once shot for the market, they are now fully protected in most parts of the United States, and the trumpeter probably will never be abundant enough to be classified as a game bird. However, whistling swans—better known as tundra swans in many regions—have been legally hunted in Utah's Great Salt Lake Valley since 1962 and in more recent years in several other western states. By the early 1980s, some hunters and many farmers in the mid-Atlantic states were clamoring for a season on tundra swans because the birds had become so numerous that they were—and are—a significant cause of crop damage where they gather in dense concentrations. Though tundra swans are beautiful and graceful birds, some long-suffering North Carolina farmers call them "sky carp." Beginning in 1984, that state opened an experimental tundra swan season with a special-permit fee and a daily limit of just one bird. Several states have followed suit, and more are likely to do so.

Each year, seasons and limits on the various waterfowl species are set by the states, within federal guidelines and narrower guidelines established by Flyway Councils. (See Chapter 6 for information on the four designated continental flyways and Chapter 13 for a discussion of waterfowl management and regulation.) Seasons and limits are based in large part on species-population censuses on the northern breeding grounds, but also on other factors such as habitat conditions on the breeding grounds, along the vast migratory corridors, and on the major wintering grounds.

Thus, the regulations may be liberal along a particular flyway with regard to a species of duck. For example, they may be looser if that species is abundant, has had a successful nesting season, and will migrate and winter in areas where hunting pressure has not been too heavy, resting waters will be sufficient, the bird's preferred foods are plentiful, and so on. But for a species of duck that shows signs of decline or stress from adverse environmental conditions, the bag limit may be skimpy and the season may be curtailed—or the season may be closed entirely until the species population becomes much larger.

Another factor is the occasional shift in the range of a species or subspecies of waterfowl. For many years, perhaps for centuries, the lesser snow goose (*Ansercaerulescens caerulescens*) was chiefly a bird of the West, migrating and wintering along the Pacific, Central, and Mississippi Flyways. Among American geese, only

A hunter jumps a very startled duck on a farm pond in Ohio. Some of the finest gunning is for puddle ducks over small waters.

Canadas are more abundant and widespread. But the greater snow goose (*A. c. altantica*) of the East was not so abundant. In fact, the Atlantic Flyway states had no open season on snows for decades. Gradually—probably because of climatic changes—lesser snows extended their range northward and eastward, and the Atlantic Flyway's populations of snow geese increased steadily. By the mid-1980s, hunters in many Atlantic Flyway states were able to bag more snows than Canadas—and the seasons and limits reflected this situation.

A wise and serious duck hunter can expand both the "hunting" season and his own pleasure by becoming an expert in waterfowl identification. In these days when seasons are either restricted or closed on some species, identification is doubly important. Identifying waterfowl can give many hours of satisfying recreation, and if you carry a camera in place of a gun, the hunting season is never closed.

There's also a possible dividend in capturing live action and rare beauty on film.

When redheads or canvasbacks or any other species is protected because of its scarcity, it is essential that a hunter identify the target before he pulls the trigger.

Knowing a mallard from a merganser has another side, too. Try cooking both at the same time and in the same manner and see which is delicious and which actually isn't fit to eat. (Contrary to widely accepted notions, a merganser can be very tasty—if you know what it is and how to prepare it.)

Let's digress a moment and see exactly what is involved in identifying ducks and geese. You can look for color and pattern of plumage, of course, and if the ducks are near enough and not in motion this is a good way. But knowing plumage and color isn't enough. Besides, many ducks wear different plumage in summer, called eclipse plumage, than they do in spring

This gunner is hunting broadbills—scaup—on Lake Ontario. His decoys are arranged so that birds will have both the room and the temptation to come in, descending against the wind. Only in rare situations can a waterfowler get away with sitting in the open, as he's doing. The trees and jumbled rocks break up his silhouette as seen from the direction of flight, but he must remain perfectly still or the birds will flare. (*Will Ryan*)

and fall. This accounts for such confusion as hunters identifying male ducks as females early in the hunting season. Often during this period drakes haven't had time to regain their "normal" plumage after summer molt.

There are other factors which confuse identification. Adult birds are likely to vary slightly from immature birds. And even chemical or mineral content of water can change a duck's color. White-breasted ducks, for example, may show up as yellow or brown after lengthy exposure to a mineral-laden pond.

The complete duck hunter does not rely on plumage alone to guide him. Instead he checks the habitat, the action or behavior, the shape or silhouette, the flying characteristics, and the voice of the bird. Some birds can be positively identified by voice—the woody, for example. Others, such as the drake pintail, can be positively identified by shape no matter what the stage of his plumage.

The antics and maneuvers of a flock of waterfowl in the air can help indicate many species. Mallards, pintails, and widgeon form loose groups. Sometimes the individual birds in a flock seem to be going in all directions at once although aiming at the same place. Teal and shovelers flash past in small, marvelously coordinated groups. Fire at them or startle them and the groups seem to explode, regrouping again soon afterward.

Mergansers often appear in single file. Canvasbacks change from wavy lines to irregular V's and back again. Redheads "boil up" in short flights from one end of a lake to another. You get the impression they are very nervous.

A good observer can often identify ducks from wingbeats, because some are merely fast and others are very, very fast. Some fly with short, rapid fluttering of the wings; others take long strokes. Even the sound of wings can be important. Canvasbacks zoom past with a steady "rush" of wings, while the pinions of goldeneyes whistle during flight. All these things become evident with experience, and it's highly rewarding experience, too.

There are few dull moments in the wonderful world of waterfowlers. Any duck or goose hunt can be high adventure. The adventure may come in the form of a sudden, savage blizzard or in the precarious punt-boat ride across a choppy bay from freezing blind to cozy clubhouse. It can come when a peregrine falcon dives down into the decoys and almost turns inside out when, too late, it discovers its mistake. The adventure may be when your dog makes a spectacular retrieve of a cripple. And it may even happen when an angry mother hippopotamus chases you from your makeshift blind beside a Tanganyika water hole. That actually happened to me.

Like Frank Sayers and millions of other addicted waterfowlers, I really do live ten days a week during open season.

CHAPTER 1

LARGE PUDDLE DUCKS

Distributed about the earth are ninety-eight forms of river and pond ducks, also called surface-feeding, dabbling, or puddle ducks. Sixteen are seen in North America if the transient European widgeon and European teal are included. A number of charcteristics separate puddle ducks from other types.

These characteristics are as follows: (1) In flushing from land or water, puddle ducks rise with a strong upward motion as if being catapulted skyward. Most other ducks patter or "run" along the surface before takeoff.

(2) Pond ducks ordinarily feed in shallow water by tipping up (with head under water) or by dabbling along the fringes of relatively small bodies of water. Their diet consists largely of vegetable matter and they rarely dive, except when injured to escape danger. On the whole, puddle ducks are excellent on the table.

(3) The legs of puddle ducks are placed nearer the middle of the body than in other waterfowl and therefore they are able to move about more freely on land than are the diving ducks and mergansers (fish-eating ducks). Also, the hind toe of puddle ducks is smaller than it is on diving ducks.

(4) The colored patch on the secondary flight feathers of the wings of puddle ducks, called the speculum, is usually more highly colored and iridescent than it is on diving ducks.

(5) Puddle ducks and divers differ from mergansers in that their bills are broad and flat, whereas mergansers have narrow and nearly cylindrical bills which are saw-toothed.

When ducks are observed feeding in grainfields, crop fields, or almost anywhere on land,

more than likely they will be puddle ducks. They are partial to ripened grain. Any ducks feeding in woods are almost certain to be puddle ducks. Mallards or wood ducks fattened on acorns are among the most highly regarded food ducks of all.

Common Mallard

Among all the ducks on earth, the common mallard is probably the most abundant. This species lives and nests throughout the entire Northern Hemisphere.

Besides being the most abundant duck, the mallard has been of greatest importance to man as well. It readily becomes domesticated, and nearly all of today's domestic breeds of ducks originated in the mallard.

In many ways the mallard is every sportsman's duck. It is not the fastest among our waterfowl on the wing, but it is very fast. It is also among the largest and most handsome of our native ducks and surely it is one of the best on the table. For these reasons and because it decoys well, but not *too* well, it is certainly the most sought after of all ducks. A handsome greenhead, appropriately named for the drake's rich iridescent green head which shows a purplish gloss in sunlight, is an elegant trophy.

Unless it is an extremely dark day, mallards are not difficult to identify in flight. When startled, they spring from the water and rise up vertically for several feet before finally leveling off in flight. When under way the head and neck are carried forward and slightly erect. The body

A peculiar characteristic of the mallard drake is the dark, jaunty little tail curl that sticks up above the white tail coverts. One of America's most handsome waterfowl, the mallard is also the most popular and widely distributed. (*Karl H. Maslowski*)

appears rather large, and the wingspread is greater than among diving ducks.

In full flight the forward and rear portions of the drake appear dark, while the breast and underwings seem to be light. Most of the time the white bars of the speculum are also evident.

The female is somewhat more difficult to identify. Sometimes the white bars of the speculum can be seen. Except for these white wing bars, however, it is easy to confuse the hen mallard with the hen pintail.

Compared to other ducks, mallards are noisy birds. They quack loudly in flight but even more

so on their feeding grounds. The male's call is a low quack that can be heard long distances. The female has a loud, resonant quack and this is what shooters hear when a flock circles around the decoys.

Mallards breed most extensively in the northwest quarter of North America. They winter throughout the United States wherever there is open water, with the greatest concentration in the lower half of the Mississippi Valley and in the Gulf states from Florida to Texas.

In early autumn mallards become restless. As early as September they begin flights from local

Though drab by comparison with the male of the species, the mallard hen is a beautiful bird. Since an abundance of nesting females is crucial to a successful reproductive season, the bag limit on hens is usually much lower than the limit on drakes. (*Wisconsin Natural Resources Department*)

nesting areas to nearby feeding grounds. But the main migration flights do not begin until late September or October. Then as the days become golden and vegetation changes color, mallards gather in huge flocks, and on sharp, frosty nights they begin their flights south.

Depending upon their location and the situation, mallards are hunted by every conceivable legal means: by shooting from fixed blinds over decoys, by jump-shooting in rivers and ponds, by waiting in grainfields, and by pass-shooting along established lines of flight.

Mallards average slightly over two and a half pounds in weight, with drakes heavier than females. Average wingspread is thirty-six inches.

Black Duck

If native North American ducks are ever ranked for wariness and intelligence, the black duck would have to win most of the prizes. At least that is the consensus of most hunters in the United States.

This handsome, large duck is similar to the mallard in many ways and has recently been

A mallard hen, startled by an approaching hunter, jumps from a brushy farmland fenceline. The hunter may be equally startled when mallards explode from cover, leaping up almost vertically. (*Nebraska Game Commission*)

reclassified as a mallard subspecies—much to the displeasure of many hunters, ornithologists, and conservationists who are concerned about its management and future. It is dark brown with white only underneath the wings. It is a swift flyer, usually at high altitudes, and is a very delicious bird on the table. Blacks are called by many local names, including black mallard, black, blackie, beef duck, brown duck, and velvet duck.

Generally the black is a bird of the eastern states, using only the Atlantic and Mississippi Flyways. It is often seen in the company of mallards, but along the Atlantic Seaboard it frequents salt marshes and brackish lagoons much more than mallards. In voice, silhouette, and habits it is very similar to the mallard, although it is far more difficult to decoy or call into shotgunning range.

The main breeding areas of the black extend from the Great Lakes vicinity northeastward to

Unusual photos of black ducks (with a few mallards mixed in) at rest on a northern Ohio pond. Blacks are very wary, shy birds.

Labrador and eastward to the Atlantic Coast. The main wintering area is in the southeastern United States.

The first autumn flights south begin early in September at roughly the same time bluewing teal begin to move. Then throughout the autumn the flights, composed of relatively small numbers of birds, increase in volume. During late autumn and winter, many black ducks are forced to salt water because freshwater ponds inland are frozen.

Because black ducks have fared poorly in recent years, seasons are often closed or limits severely reduced. It is therefore essential to recognize them in flight. There is some chance to confuse the black duck with the hen mallard, but ordinarily blacks are darker in color. On dull days they appear to be solid black and gray under the wings. In addition, the two white bars of the mallard's speculum are missing in the black duck. Hunters also confuse scoters with blacks because they have similar color and are abundant in the same general areas of the Atlantic Seaboard. However, scoters have larger heads and shorter necks.

The average black duck weighs over two and a half pounds and the wingspread is about thirty-six inches for adult birds.

American Pintail

It is difficult for most dedicated waterfowlers to discuss the pintail without becoming almost lyrical. Also known as the sprig, it is an extremely elegant, graceful bird, both on the water and in flight. Anyone who has hunted often in pintail country has thrilled to the zigzagging maneuvers at great heights before the birds finally descend, perhaps among the hunter's decoys.

The drake has a long pointed tail, a white collar, and a dark brown head which changes from purple to pink to green in certain kinds of sunlight. By contrast, the female is a drab light brown and lacks the long tail. These birds have the widest breeding range of all our ducks.

The main breeding range of the American pintail includes the northwest quarter of the United States, all the western half of Canada, and Alaska. The wintering area covers all the coastal regions of the United States, all of Mexico and Central America, and extends into northern South America.

On the water pintails are very nervous birds and seem always on the alert, and ready to take alarm. When surprised, they bounce vertically upward and often bunch closely as they rise— which means they furnish an unusual target for gunners. Pintails usually approach decoys from a great height and then circle warily, as if looking for unnatural movement below. If they are satisfied that all is safe, they will plunge down quickly among the decoys. Otherwise they will turn and hurry away.

In autumn, pintails are among the early migrants. They are often found in the first bags of the season, usually with teal and locally born mallards and black ducks. Although pintails are taken by hunters in all four flyways, they are most abundant in the Pacific and Central Flyways. In recent years, pintail populations have declined significantly, and their restoration is among the goals of the North American Waterfowl Management Plan.

There is great difference of opinion among the most experienced duck hunters on the intelligence of pintails. Perhaps the best way to describe them is to say that they are highly erratic. On some days they seem to plunge into the decoys with great abandon. On other days it's practically impossible to decoy them.

Pintail males average over two pounds each; hens go just under two pounds. The average wingspread is thirty-four inches.

Gadwall

Although the gadwall probably has a wider world distribution than any other duck, South America and Australia being the only two places where it is not found, it really isn't plentiful anywhere. In North America it is primarily a bird of the western and central regions. In these regions it may be reasonably plentiful in certain isolated localities but absent in nearby localities. Even though it is an easy duck to identify, it is often confused with the female pintail and the young drake pintail, with which it frequently associates.

While resting on the water, gadwalls appear as medium to fairly small gray-brown ducks with pale heads. At a distance and in poor light

When feeding or at rest, a mingling of species is fairly common among puddle ducks. The bird in the foreground is a pintail drake; behind it are black ducks.

The pintail hen is less colorful than the male and has a shorter tail, but is still easy to identify. Pintails are great flyers and excellent on the table. (*Karl H. Maslowski*)

they may resemble black ducks. On the water they are more likely to be in company with other ducks, especially baldpates and pintails, than in a flock composed entirely of gadwalls. In flight these neutral-colored birds move in small, compact flocks very swiftly and usually on a direct course. The body appears to be slender as a pintail's and the wingbeat is rapid.

Since the gadwall is the only puddle duck with a completely and conspicuously white speculum toward the back of the wing, this is the mark to look for in passing birds. Remember, though, that the baldpate also has white on the wing, but it is on the forepart. Sometimes the black rump of the male gadwall will be noticeable in flight and this is another way to identify the species. While flying or on the water, drakes often make a whistling and cack-cacking noise. Hens quack in a manner similar to mallards, although it is much softer.

Of all the puddle ducks, the gadwall is the one most likely to be seen diving rather than tipping up for food. However, this is not a common occurrence. The bird walks very well and on occasion may feed in grainfields and nearby woods.

Gadwalls breed in the northwestern United States and southwestern Canada. Their wintering area is concentrated from California and the Gulf Coast southward to central Mexico. Hunters are likely to see them at any time during the fall migration.

Male gadwalls average two pounds; females less than two pounds. Average wingspread is about thirty-three inches.

Baldpate (Widgeon)

The baldpate is another of those ducks with many names. Among them are widgeon, American widgeon, bald-headed widgeon, northern widgeon, bald duck, French teal, gray duck, robber duck, whistler, and whitebelly. However,

This drake is a baldpate, also widely known as the American widgeon (and widgeon is its preferred ornithological name). Its pale skullcap is distinctive. (*Karl H. Maslowski*)

baldpate and widgeon are most widely used, with the former coming from the white top of the head on the drakes.

Many American gunners do not rate bald-pates very highly, but I have enjoyed some memorable days with them in the marshes around the western shore of Lake Erie and con-sider baldpates extremely fine game and good table birds as well. They fly swiftly in small, compact flocks and in irregular formation. They seldom fly directly from one place to another but instead make twists and turns and other fancy maneuvers that make shooting on a windy day extremely exciting.

Baldpates rest nervously on the water with chest lower and tail higher than some other puddle ducks. They quickly take alarm and then jump vertically into the air, making a rat-tling sound with their wings. In flight the flocks are fairly easily recognized by the conspicuous markings of the male. For example, there is the white crown on the head and the white breast. However, after spending time in certain kinds of water, baldpates may have yellow and even brown breasts, discolored by the water.

Females also have white breasts, whitish wing patches, and gray underwing surfaces. This is similar to the female gadwall except that the baldpate hen has no white in the speculum.

The American wildfowler is treated to many wild and primeval sounds, such as the sigh of a northeast wind and the yelps and honking of geese. Just as exciting is the wild, musical note of the male baldpate as it passes by a blind and carefully examines the decoys. The female's cry is much louder and also more coarse, and her quack of alarm really seems to express terror.

Among the nicknames for the baldpate is rob-ber duck. Through a spotting scope one day, I watched a number of baldpates mixed in among a larger number of canvasbacks and redheads. The cans and redheads would dive and bring vegetation to the surface, at which point a bald-pate would immediately snatch it away. Since baldpates cannot dive very well, this is a com-mon way of obtaining food. But in payment, they warn the dimmer-witted redheads and canvasbacks when danger approaches.

Early in the season baldpates come very read-ily to decoys. And curiosity causes younger birds especially to return again and again to look over the decoys even after hunters have fired at them.

A close relative of the baldpate is the Euro-pean widgeon. European and American wid-geon are similar in size, averaging one and a half pounds. Average wingspread is thirty-three inches.

CHAPTER 2

SMALL PUDDLE DUCKS

Bluewing Teal

The little bluewing teal, exclusively a resident of the New World, is very fast and among the most difficult winged targets of the world. He's handsome, too, and is my favorite both on the wing and in the broiler.

This species is a very early migrant. The small, compact flocks of bluewings leave northern nesting grounds early in September or sometimes even in August and have passed southward often before waterfowl seasons are well under way. If the timing is right, sportsmen will have shooting on the first few days of the season.

It is hard to describe the exciting flight of bluewings. Small flocks, which may average from five to fifteen birds, dart swiftly, often very low over the marshes, twisting and dodging around trees and bushes. There is no predicting where they are going and when they will get there. You can hear their uniquely twittering calls in flight as they approach. When a shot is fired, the birds in the flock seem to explode and dart away in all directions, but quickly regroup and continue their flight. Often enough to make it very interesting, they will swing around and pass over the blind a second or a third time. This doesn't mean that even an experienced shooter will bag enough birds for dinner. (Bear in mind that teal have been called "breakfast ducks" owing to their small size.)

On the water the bluewing teal appears very small, but size alone is not a good identifying feature because the silhouette resembles some of the larger puddle ducks. Perhaps the best distinguishing features are the blue wing patches of both sexes and the white crescent-shaped cheek markings of the male. At close range this white cheek patch is especially noticeable, as is the white patch on each flank near the base of the tail.

Unless the light is good enough to reveal the blue wing patch, the female bluewing teal is extremely difficult to distinguish from the female greenwing and the cinnamon teal. The female shoveler is also similar in appearance except for her slightly larger size and unique bill. On the water, bluewings seldom tip up while feeding. Instead, they collect small bits of vegetation on the surface or just under the surface in water only a few inches deep.

Unlike many puddle ducks, bluewings are silent while feeding. But while flying, drakes utter a whistling peep that is often repeated and then a soft lisping note that at a distance may be confused with that of the wood duck. Females utter only a faint quack and this less often than the quacking of many other ducks. When feeding, bluewings usually remain in close groups so that they almost seem to be touching one another.

The breeding area of bluewing teal covers nearly all the plains and pothole country of the western United States and Canada. The wintering area extends from the southern United States, particularly Florida and the Louisiana delta country, through Cuba, Puerto Rico, Mexico, and southward far into South America.

As early as August, bluewings in the northern pothole country stir and become restless. By the

These birds are a hen (foreground) and drake bluewing teal. The drake is easily identified by the white crescent on its cheek. (*Maslowski & Goodpaster*)

end of August many of the mature males fly south, and the waterfowler who doesn't go afield for reconnaissance before opening day never even sees them. Then in September the females and birds of the year (the traditional term for birds less than a year old) also begin their migration southward.

The speed and agility of bluewings in flight is so amazing that they have been given credit for attaining speeds of ninety miles an hour. Of course, such speeds are vastly overestimated, but these tiny teal have established some amazing speed and endurance records. A teal banded in Quebec, Canada, on September 5 was killed on October 2 in British Guiana, a direct airline distance of 2,400 miles from the point where it was banded. This bird had flown at least eighty-five miles a day, perhaps against strong winds, for twenty-eight days.

Greenwing Teal

Next to the wood duck, most outdoorsmen will agree that the greenwing teal is the most beautiful North American duck. When resting in the sun on a calm pond, it has been described as resembling a delicate porcelain duck.

Being the smallest of the North American ducks, the greenwing can easily be distinguished from any except the other teals and the buffleheads. Greenwings usually appear shorter in the body and have shorter necks than bluewings. But as in identifying other ducks, size alone is unreliable. While resting on ponds and small lakes, which are likely places to find them, greenwings seem to be much less nervous than some other ducks. It isn't unusual to see them loafing on sandbars, beaches or mud flats, where they often sit preening and sunning.

A greenwing teal drake. Greenwings are among our smallest ducks and, like all teal, they fly erratically and make tricky targets. (*Karl H. Maslowski*)

The flight of the greenwing is very similar to that of the bluewing, fast and erratic. Teal have a habit of wheeling and circling together in a dense flock, as do domestic pigeons. During flight the wings make a whistling sound.

The breeding range of the greenwing teal extends farther north than that of the bluewing. Its center of greatest abundance is in the huge prairie areas of western Canada. The limit of the breeding range extends northward to the Arctic Circle and includes a large part of Alaska.

Fall migrations begin with the first cold weather. But instead of hurrying south as rapidly as the bluewings, greenwings often stop and linger wherever they find attractive feeding and where they can be undisturbed. Then, when deep cold and snowstorms arrive, the greenwings suddenly disappear, and the next time anyone sees them they are in warmer latitudes. The greenwing's main wintering area consists of the southern third of the United States and most of the northern half of Mexico, where good shooting continues in winter.

A duck of inland sloughs, marshes, and slow-moving streams, the greenwing feeds by reaching down to sift food from muddy bottoms or to pluck weeds in very shallow places. Characteristically it feeds by tipping up, and it is common to see this duck kicking its feet in the air to maintain its equilibrium. Among the most active ducks on land, it can run quickly, and occasionally wanders far from the water in search of berries, acorns, and wild grain.

Greenwings decoy rather easily. Often they will make low passes time and again across a spread of decoys before finally dropping into them. Particularly early in the season, they may rise, circle uncertainly, and drop in a second

Greenwing teal rising from the water at Amchitka Island, Alaska. This is a productive nesting region for greenwings. (*Jerry L. Hout*)

time after having been shot at previously. Roasted, baked, or broiled, greenwings are just as delicious on the table as their close cousins the bluewings.

Cinnamon Teal

The cinnamon teal is the only North American puddle duck which is confined in range to the western portion of the continent. This is a familiar bird to sportsmen along the Pacific Flyway and to some extent to those on the Central Flyway.

This teal is distinct in another way in that there are two separate populations in the New World. One exists in western North America as described above, and the other lives in southern South America. The closest distance between the two is about 2,000 miles.

Cinnamon teal are birds of tule-bordered, shallow edges of lakes and marshes from Alaska south to California. Not nearly as gregarious as other puddle ducks, they are seldom found in large flocks. Once the breeding season has passed, they are mostly encountered in pairs or family groups.

Breeding range of the cinnamon teal is pretty much confined to the western third of the United States plus a portion of British Columbia and Alberta. The winter range is that portion of the southwestern United States and Mexico just south of the breeding range. The autumn migration of cinnamon teal is really just a shift southward that begins early in September and continues through October. During that shift southward, West Coast gunners are furnished with considerable action.

In flight the cinnamon teal is difficult to distinguish from bluewings and greenwings, except that in good light they have a distinctly red color and they do have blue wing patches on both sexes.

Among the most trusting of North American waterfowl, cinnamon teal are often slow to take alarm. When frightened, however, they burst into the air vertically and disappear by flying low and erratically over the marshlands. They are very silent birds, especially in flight. Occasionally the male utters a low rattling or chattering sound which never carries very far. The female has only a simple, soft quack.

Shoveler

The shoveler superficially resembles the mallard, but is much smaller and in many ways bears a close resemblance to the teal.

The shoveler is known by a number of colorful names, including spoonbill, shovel duck, shovelhead, laughing mallard, scooper duck, dipper duck, mud duck, French teal, spoonbill teal, and broadbill.

At first glance the green head of the male shoveler does suggest the drake mallard. However, the oversize bill shaped like a spatula immeditely separates this bird from any other North American waterfowl. Even at a considerable distance the shoveler isn't too hard to distinguish from other puddle ducks. The male sits low on the water with his bill tilted down-

ward. He also shows more white on his body. The female is plain brown, as are many other ducks, but the shoveler hen has the same flat head and large bill as the male. This is easy to distinguish on the water or in flight.

Mostly, shovelers are encountered in pairs or small flocks. When startled, their flight somewhat resembles that of teal, since it is erratic and has frequent downward plunges. However, shovelers are in no way as fast flyers as any of the teals. They can rise vertically from the water with a noisy rattling of wings; they can also alight almost vertically with scarcely a splash.

Shovelers have small throats and correspondingly weak voices. The male utters a low grunting sound and the female has a feeble quack. But even these sounds are seldom heard by duck hunters.

An interesting fact about the shoveler is that some of them annually make the 2,000-mile flight from Alaska to the Hawaiian Islands. Alaska is an important breeding area and Hawaii is an important wintering area.

Among all the puddle ducks, the shoveler probably ranks lowest as a game bird. It decoys easily, maybe too easily, and most shovelers are scrawny, providing skimpy meat. However, there are some exceptions. In many parts of their wintering area, as in Mexico where food is abundant, shovelers can grow fat and delectable.

A main point to remember about shovelers is that they dearly love warm weather. Southerly migrations begin early in September and usually are finished a month later. Their main winter habitat is in warm, shallow inland waters.

Wood Duck

Maybe you know this exquisite waterfowl by such names as summer duck, bride, canard du bois, squealer, swamp duck, or wood widgeon, all common names in scattered parts of America. Even the scientific name of this bird—Aix sponsa—translates into "wedding dress," which neatly describes the beautiful plumage of the male.

The wood duck is not really a puddle species, but we will describe it here for convenience and because in many respects it resembles the teal and its habits are often similar.

The shoveler drake superficially resembles a mallard drake, but note its very large, spatula-shaped bill and white breast. (*Karl H. Maslowski*)

The male woody is a striking character no matter whether you find him on the water, perched in a tree, or flying swiftly past. The easiest characteristics to identify are the white-striped, crested head, the white throat, and the dark chest and body. Both drake and hen sit proudly on the water, floating lightly with head and tail erect as if very much on the alert. The most noticeable characteristic of the female is a white ring around the eye and a pale or white throat patch. Otherwise the female appears to be a drab gray bird. The flight of the woody is swift, strong, and direct to its target. Because of the white underparts, an observer who doesn't have a very good look at the bird may easily confuse it with a baldpate.

Years ago, the population of wood ducks across America reached a low point. Perhaps this can be blamed on the woody's trait of nesting in cavities of trees. As more forests and woodlots were cleared, the number of nesting trees diminished. In recent years, however, waterfowl biologists have devised all sorts of artificial nest boxes, and have succeeded in restoring the population of these birds. Woodies are now so populous in some areas that gunners are encouraged to hunt them in order to lighten pressure on mallards and sprig.

The typical routine of the woody is to rest during the night on open ponds or pools, preferably in woodlands. Then in the early morning it flies out to feed in wild-rice marshes, swamps, along the banks or shores of streams, or in other ponds.

The drake wood duck is America's gaudiest and most beautiful of waterfowl. It's also a great flyer and delicious on the table. (*Karl. H. Maslowski*)

A woodie hen, peering from her tree-cavity nest. A depletion of woodland habitat has recurrently threatened the future of this species, but in recent decades the shortage of tree hollows has been alleviated in large part by man-made nesting boxes.

The swift flight of a woody can be all the more exciting because the bird frequents wooded streams and ponds. It can fly through the thickest timber with ease, darting quickly to avoid tree limbs and vegetation.

Found almost everywhere, but most numerous in the Mississippi Flyway, the woody is a rather noisy bird. It is especially noisy when feeding in the woods, where it squeals, clucks, whistles, or squeaks continually. Probably the sound most familiar to sportsmen is the *whoo-eek, whoo-eek* which the bird utters when it senses danger, as when passing close to a duck blind or spotting a hunter from overhead.

The woody is a grand table bird, rated second only to the bluewing and greenwing teal.

This photo represents one of the author's treasured memories. It shows Bauer holding up a brace of baldpates bagged on a shallow marsh at the western end of Lake Erie.

Ruddy Duck

The ruddy duck is not a true puddle duck, but since it normally dwells in a pond or puddle environment, it will be considered in this chapter for convenience. The ruddy is handsome, but not an especially great game bird. It flies well once it completes the laborious chore of getting aloft, although normally it prefers not to fly at all. Curious and somewhat comical in appearance, it is exclusively a North American species.

The number of nicknames used for the ruddy is longer than those for any other duck. A few of the more interesting local names would include booby, booby coot, bristletail, broadbill dipper, bullneck, bumblebee coot, butterball, dicky duck, dipper duck, dumpling duck, dummy duck, hardhead, hickory head, leatherback, little soldier, mud dipper, muskrat duck, paddywack, quilltail coot, rudder bird, rudder duck, shot pouch, shanty duck, sleeping booby, sleepy coot, spatter duck, spiketail, spoonbill, stifftail, stiffie, and wiretail.

No matter whether in bright summer plumage or in dark winter dress, the male ruddy can be quickly identified by its erect, fan-shaped tail and its pure white cheeks overset by a dark skullcap. It also has a bright blue, quite broad mandible. The body is distinctively short and stubby.

After pattering along the water surface for a long distance before clearing it, the bird has a jerky, uneven flight. It appears to be tail-heavy and there is considerable beating of wings during takeoff. Both male and female are usually silent during flight.

Ruddies nest in central Canada and the plains states. They winter along our warmer coasts and into Mexico. Autumn migration begins in September and usually follows the main courses of streams and lakes. Most literature states that the birds fly low and in large flocks. However, in many years and on a number of flyways, I have never seen any very large concentration of ruddy ducks. Probably the longest flights are made early in the morning or after dusk.

Other ducks that American gunners might encounter, especially if they hunt along our southern border and in Mexico, are the masked duck, the black-bellied tree duck, and the fulvous tree duck. But none of these birds ventures far north of the border, and so they are not important in this discussion. Nor do they belong rightfully to the classification of puddle duck. Still other puddle ducks, such as the European teal and European widgeon, occasionally stray to this continent during migration, but are seldom encountered by American waterfowlers.

CHAPTER 3

DIVING DUCKS AND SEA DUCKS

More often than not our diving ducks frequent the larger, deeper lakes and rivers plus coastal marshes, lagoons, and inlets. This is not a hard-and-fast rule, but normally they feed more by diving than do puddle ducks, and they can feed this way at considerable depths. To escape danger they can travel great distances under water.

More than forty species of diving ducks exist, and twenty of these are found at one time or another in North America.

The diving ducks lack the brilliant speculums of most puddle ducks, but there are important field marks in most species. Since most have small tails, their huge paddle feet may be used as rudders in flight and are often visible to good observers. When launching into flight, most of

A typical cold-weather scene on a Lake Erie reef. Although the decoys were puddle-duck imitations, they attracted buffleheads and scaup within gunshot.

this group patter along the water before becoming airborne.

Since their wings are small in proportion to the size and weight of their bodies, they have a very rapid wingbeat when compared to puddle ducks. This is an important aspect of waterfowl identification throughout the country.

Canvasback

To many the canvasback is the greatest game bird in the world, both because of its speed on the wing and because of its high reputation among epicures. Canvasbacks are among our easiest birds to identify. First, they are quite large. Second, even at a considerable distance the long bill and elongated head will distinguish them from redheads, with which they often join company. However, the best means of identification is the extreme whiteness of the drake's back. The female, although darker than the drake, has the same general outline of head and body. All canvasbacks sit low on the water. When about to dive, the species lunges upward and forward as if to launch itself into the descent.

In flight the main recognition marks of the canvasback are its large size, white body, and long, slender neck and dark head. The wings are long and pointed but of small surface compared to the large body. It is miraculous that wings of this size can give such terrific speed and suggest such great power in flight. Canvasbacks migrate in formations which constantly shift between wavy lines and regular V's. Smaller flocks occasionally fly in irregular, compact bunches.

The main breeding grounds of canvasbacks are on the western Canadian prairie extending far to the north. There is also a small breeding area in Alaska. Canvasbacks winter all along our Pacific Coast and down through the western half of Mexico. They also winter along our Atlantic Coast from New York southward to Louisiana, and along the Gulf Coast of Mexico. Ordinarily the bird is a late migrant, and it often stays in the North until freezing water and heavy snowstorms drive it south.

Canvasback shooting is probably never better than during a bad storm, when the birds move downwind at incredible speeds. The most famous wintering area for canvasbacks is the region along the coast of Virginia and North Carolina. They gather there in the company of other diving ducks to feed on the roots, seeds, grass, and other vegetation which is especially to their liking.

The delicate and delicious flavor of canvasbacks is praised wherever waterfowlers gather. It could be attributed to the species' liking of wild celery buds and the fact that wild celery in some areas furnishes a great part of the canvasback's diet. This isn't necessarily true, because on the Pacific Coast, where wild celery is not found, canvasbacks rely to a great extent upon a plant called wapatoo, and there the flesh is just as delicious. However, canvasbacks have occasionally been known to gorge on the rotting flesh of spawned-out salmon, and when they do so they are not fit to eat.

Sometimes the canvasback is a most wary bird and very difficult to approach. But in early autumn the young birds and the new southern arrivals usually decoy easily. Once they have encountered shooting, they rapidly become more shy and then must be considered among the most clever of our native waterfowl.

Cans have suffered hard times in recent years as a result of prolonged droughts, pollutants, shrinking winter habitat, and related factors. Along the Mississippi and East Coast, formerly the mecca for canvasback gunning, they are often stricken from the legal game list—that is, the season is closed. Fortunately, the populations on the West Coast have not been as severely depleted. As with all game, however, you must check your state's regulations with regard to current seasons and limits. Through protection, habitat enlargement and enhancement, and other methods of modern wildlife management, game biologists hope to rebuild the eastern canvasback populations, though it seems doubtful that they can ever be restored to their former enormous numbers.

Redhead

The redhead, or American pochard, ranges from the Atlantic to the Pacific Coast and is often found with the canvasback, which it somewhat resembles. But on closer inspection, only the red-brown color of the male's head and

A drake redhead. Both redheads and canvasbacks are members of the pochard family, and they look somewhat alike. But they can be distinguished even in flight because redheads appear shorter and darker than cans, the head-and-bill contours are different, and redheads fly more erratically. (*Karl H. Maslowski*)

the neutral color of the female's body are similar. The male redhead has a puffy, round dark head and chest and a grayish body, whereas the canvasback's body shows up as almost pure white. Once you've observed redheads on the water and in flight—and especially if you've seen them together with canvasbacks—you should be able to tell the species apart. But because canvasbacks are occasionally mistaken for redheads, the same regulations sometimes apply to both. If the canvasback limit is reduced or the season closed, you may find that gunning for redheads is also curtailed in a given area. In some regions, redheads may also be protected because their own numbers have dwindled, though at the time of this writing they can be bagged along some flyways where the canvasback season is closed.

Redheads tend to gather in very large rafts and to spend the days on deep, open water. Only bad storms break up these rafts into smaller groups and drive them into smaller-water areas. They do fly out regularly in the morning and evening to feed in shallower places.

The redhead's main nesting area lies in central Canada and the north-central United States. This fact no doubt has contributed much to its decrease in recent years. Too much of the land normally in the redhead's breeding range has been drained and otherwise used for agricultural purposes.

Wintering areas for the redhead are widely separated. One concentration is located along the coasts of Virginia and North Carolina. The other wintering area includes the coast of California, the Texas and Louisiana Gulf Coast plus the northern half of Mexico. These handsome ducks migrate between summer and winter areas in V-shaped, fairly regular flocks. But during movements from resting to feeding grounds during the day, they move in much larger flocks and in an irregular formation. This is the way hunters will ordinarily see them.

While flying, redheads appear shorter and darker than canvasbacks. The wings seem to beat more rapidly and the flight seems more erratic. They arise from the water in a confused manner and always appear to be in a hurry. Often when rafting or resting on open water the flock will suddenly boil up for no apparent reason and then just as quickly settle down again.

Male redheads make very little sound except an occasional soft purring which resembles that of a cat. Occasionally in autumn, males may also give a weak quack-quack. Females are much noisier and when flushed from the water they make a loud, clear quack which is higher in tone than the quack of a mallard or black duck.

The main autumn migration from nesting to wintering area is well under way during October. Sometimes they travel in company with canvasbacks and somtimes with scaup, and on other occasions they travel alone. Occasionally, migrating flocks will pause in the Great Lakes area and linger there all winter long if ice does not cover the entire lake surface. The redhead is just as good and can be just as bad on the table as a canvasback. No doubt this is a matter of the bird's diet.

Greater Scaup

The greater scaup is a handsome, sturdy bird and a strong, fast flyer. Probably its name is derived from its habit of feeding around oyster and mussel beds, which in Europe and Scotland are called scaup beds. It may also have been named for its characteristic cry of *scaup-scaup*.

In much of the United States the greater scaup is known as the bluebill or lake bluebill. It is also called the broadbill. But by any name it is very similar to the lesser scaup and it is very difficult to distinguish between the two in the field. The greater scaup weighs slightly more than the lesser scaup. Also the gloss of the nearly black head of the greater scaup tends to be green as compared to the purple gloss in a lesser scaup.

Virtually the entire breeding range of the

A drake greater scaup, also known as the broadbill or bluebill. (*Karl H. Maslowski*)

greater scaup is confined to Alaska and the Yukon Territory. Two separate wintering areas exist, one along our northern Pacific Coast and the other along the Atlantic Coast from New England south to North Carolina. A number of birds also winter in the eastern Great Lakes region. On the wintering grounds, greater scaup prefer the larger bodies of water, where they ordinarily gather in huge rafts during the daytime. Rough or choppy water doesn't seem to bother them; in fact, they seem to enjoy it.

Scaup travel from place to place in rather compact formations, and their flight is rapid. The wings produce a loud rustling sound and if it is a very large flock this sound is almost a roar. During longer migrations they have been observed by pilots at very high altitudes. But when traveling between feeding areas, they normally fly very low. A good way to distinguish the greater scaup from the lesser scaup in flight is the longer light strip which shows through the wing.

Of all ducks, the greater scaup is one of the most difficult to kill. Gunners who are not good marksmen or who shoot at these birds at long range lose far too many of them. Unless a scaup is mortally hit on the first shot it will dive repeatedly and never come up again until it is far away from the shooter. They are also better able to elude retrievers than most other ducks, which cannot dive so well.

When resting on the sea or a large lake, greater scaup often sit in an unbroken line parallel to the coast or shore. Suddenly a bird at one end of the line will take wing, and it will be followed in order right along the line to the last bird. To see this maneuver in the distance is to be almost certain that you have seen a flock of greater scaup.

Greater scaup are late migrants and they seem to thrive on storms and high winds. Some of the best shooting I can recall occurred on mornings when the bluebills were flying into very stiff winds. The birds would swarm downwind, turn suddenly, bank, and slip almost without motion into the decoys.

Lesser Scaup

Lesser scaup, or little bluebills, are lively and restless ducks whether on the water or in the air. They often swim about or flush for no apparent reason. They migrate very late and often move south just ahead of freeze-up. On local flights they travel in closely bunched flocks that dart erratically, twisting and turning often. On long migration flights they stay fairly high.

This handsome species is exclusively a North American duck and it is widely distributed across the continent. It tends more to inland lakes, ponds, and marshes than other divers, although it does winter along all of our sea-coasts. Many bluebills go beyond the continental United States to winter in Mexico, Cuba, Puerto Rico, and other points south.

The nesting range of lesser scaup includes most of the Dakotas and western and north-western Canada, extending into Alaska. Next to whitewing scoters, they are the latest breeders of all continental waterfowl. Their broods do not hatch until early in July, and since ten or eleven weeks are necessary before the young are able to fly, the autumn migration is very late.

Bluebills are not held in the highest regard as food by some sportsmen. But birds taken at inland points early in the season invariably are tender and do not have the fishy taste which is sometimes associated with them.

Since the lesser scaup is a relatively abundant duck, it furnishes tremendous sport for American gunners.

Ringneck Duck

The ringneck duck, which has a ring around its bill rather than around its neck, is another species with many local names. Among these

Lesser scaup, two males and a female. (*Karl H. Maslowski*)

The handsome drake ringneck duck. Its color and the shape of the head make this one fairly easy to identify. (*Irene Vandermolen*)

are blackhead, blackjack, buckeye, foul duck, moonbill, mud duck, ringbill, ringbill shuffler, and priest duck. Although the drake has a faint, narrow chestnut collar, this marking cannot be seen in flight. Unfortunately, therefore, the name ringneck is misleading. By any name it is a handsome bird and one which is fairly easy to identify both in flight and on the water.

The male appears as a very black duck but with gray flanks that seem almost white. A white crescent at the lower part of the wing is noticeable at very long distances. Perhaps it is because the rest of the duck is so dark, but at closer ranges the white rings on the bill can also be easily noticed.

In the air, ringnecks travel in rather small flocks usually of less than a dozen birds in an open formation, and they go swiftly and directly toward their target. They usually alight without circling and surprise many hunters by dropping so suddenly into the decoys. On the wing they can be mistaken for scaup and redheads. The females are easily confused with the females of other diving species.

More than any other divers, ringnecks are essentially an inland species, being most abundant in the interior of the United States. They greatly prefer sloughs, marshes, and lagoons to open lakes. Like scaup, however, they are very nervous and alert birds. Extremely good divers, they can obtain food in water as deep as forty feet and have been captured by accident in the nets of fishermen at this depth. Although they must run along the surface of the water in the manner of all divers during takeoff, the actual rise is accomplished with much greater ease than with the other diving ducks. Ringnecks make an unmistakable whistle of the wings as they flush and as they fly past a blind.

The main nesting area extends from northern Minnesota and the upper Great Lakes into south-central Canada. The greatest migration begins during the middle of October, before the scaup's, and ends in November. By that time most nesting birds have passed southward over the Canadian border and are well on their way toward wintering areas. They winter chiefly in the southeast quarter of the United States. Another smaller area is located in northern California and Oregon.

Ringnecks are not especially shy or intelligent ducks. They have an unfortunate habit of returning again and again to a pond, even after having encountered shooters there on earlier trips. On the table the ringneck must rank with the finest of all ducks. The meat is delicious and tender, and most ringnecks are extremely fat when taken in the early fall. Ringneck hens are largely silent and males make a soft purring noise.

Goldeneye (Whistler)

The American goldeneye is another species with many names. Among these are brasseye, whistler, bright-eye, copperhead, fiddler duck, ice duck, ironhead, little diver, oyster duck, pie duck, pied whistler, sleepy diver, whistle diver, whistle duck, and winter duck.

Toward the tag end of the waterfowl season in many areas, the goldeneye furnishes all the shooting that is left after other birds have passed on southward. On the wing it is a fast and often elusive target.

Goldeneyes are wary birds, and while they will come in to decoys, they have a habit of shying away just before they are in range. On other maddening occasions they will fly in toward the decoys and then alight on the water beyond the rig. Then other birds will join them.

Small dark-headed ducks with white patches on the cheeks, American goldeneyes breed and nest completely across Canada from Newfoundland to Alaska and the Bering Sea. Their winter range is everywhere in the United States except the Southwest and the extreme Southeast. They do not mind extremely cold weather, and any lake which is not completely frozen over is a potential winter resting site for these handsome little birds.

The common nickname of whistler comes from the distinctive whistling sound of wings when the bird is in flight. Ordinarily they move in small flocks, often high in the air. When they rise from the water, they rise in rapid spirals. They are usually exceedingly wary, but on float trips for jump-shooting ducks on Ohio rivers, it has been easy to drift within a few feet of goldeneyes.

Although both male and female are usually quiet birds, drakes can utter a piercing *spear-spear* sound. Hens have only a low quack.

A close cousin of the American goldeneye

A Labrador retriever fetches a bufflehead drake.

exists only west of the Rocky Mountains. It is the Barrow's goldeneye and differs only in that it has a white crescent in front of the eye of the male. It isn't very abundant and is not very important to hunters.

Bufflehead

Here is another species peculiar to North America. Originally it was called buffalo head (and buffalo duck) because of the unusual shape of its head, but this has been reduced to bufflehead. The duck is also known as butterball. Only slightly larger than teal, bufflehead are among the world's smallest ducks. The male appears as largely white with an enormous black head marked with a triangular white crest. It can be confused with a male hooded merganser but the silhouette of the two birds is entirely different. The bufflehead is short and stubby.

Many sportsmen believe the bufflehead is not worth hunting, but shooters during late season around the Lake Erie islands have found that this bird has many sporting qualities. It flies low to the water, is fast, and has rapid wingbeats. It travels in small flocks and can flush straight up to become airborne. A very late migrant, it will remain as far north as open water permits. Ordinarily silent, drake buffleheads may give a squeaking call, and they also have a low guttural note. Hens quack very weakly.

Old Squaw

This unique and handsome bird is known only to a few shooters along the upper Atlantic Coast, in the Puget Sound area, and in the Great Lakes region. Although it is the most expert diver among native ducks, it is not very wary. It is worth noting, however, that they have been found in commercial fishing nets as deep as one hundred feet. The male old squaw can be identified instantly at any time of year by its long tail. In winter the male plumage is generally piebald, mostly white with white head and neck. In summer it is mostly brown with brown head and neck. The male sits very low on the water with his head erect and his tail well elevated. It isn't possible to confuse this duck with a pintail, which also has a long tail, because the old squaw is much more chunky of build.

Extremely garrulous birds, old squaws utter a variety of hard-to-describe cries—howls, hoots, whistles, yodels, and honks. Their common name originated as a comment on their talkativeness.

They are easily enticed by decoys, for they seem to be very trusting and full of curiosity. This makes them very easy targets. However, some old squaws seem almost immune to shot, and unless the bird is killed outright it is difficult to retrieve. To pursue a slightly wounded bird is almost useless because of its incredible diving ability.

Mergansers

Mergansers are fish-eating ducks which do not, strictly speaking, belong within the diving-duck group. They are held in low esteem, sometimes called "trash ducks," but quite often they go into a mixed bag, especially on days when the more glamorous species offer slow shooting.

All three of this continent's merganser species—the American, hooded, and red-breasted merganser—are found from coast to coast, although one variety or another may be more or less abundant in some regions. Far less gregar-

ious than other ducks, they are seen singly, in twos or threes, or occasionally in small, irregular groups. Mergansers of all varieties have long, narrow, "saw-toothed" bills (red on the American and red-breasted species, blackish on the hooded merganser) and all of them can emit croaks and grunts but are usually silent. They are long-bodied, streamlined birds, easy to recognize.

Since they are merely incidental additions to the game bag, they do not merit separate descriptions here, but it is nevertheless true that hunters should be able to identify every kind of duck they are likely to encounter. On some occasions, you might want to recognize a merganser precisely in order to hold your fire; on other occasions you might want to bring down a passing merganser in order to add a "low-point" bird to the bag rather than one of the more coveted ducks on which the daily limit is small. The surest and most enjoyable way to master field recognition is to get out there often and pack along one of the numerous field guides or waterfowl-identification charts or booklets. Some are more comprehensive than others, but most are excellent—including those issued for the Fish and Wildlife Service by the U.S. Government Printing Office.

Although mergansers are not a gourmet's delight, knowledgeable gunners ignore stories of their inedibility. In New England, where the name "coot" is often used for scoter, a "coot stew" may well contain scoter, old squaw, and merganser. The chapter on cookery will include tips on rendering such birds tasty.

Eiders and Scoters

There is some question as to which birds should be legitimately classified as "marine" or "maritime." Some authoritative and useful reference books include the bufflehead, American goldeneye, and old squaw—grouped here with the diving ducks—and also the mergansers, particularly the red-breasted merganser. Many also list the very pretty little harlequin duck, essentially a marine carnivore found on the Atlantic and Pacific coasts, but relatively scarce, less palatable than most ducks, and of little importance to the hunter.

The major sea ducks are the scoters and, to a

Mergansers are hardy and adaptable birds, though often scorned or maligned by waterfowlers. This hooded merganser nested in a box erected for wood ducks by the Maine Fish & Game Department. (*Tom Shoener, Maine Fish & Game Department*)

smaller extent, the eiders. All of these birds are characterized by thick, heavily nailed bills; on the eiders, a leathery extension on the upper mandible runs onto the forehead, while the scoters have a knob or mound on the upper mandible. The odd bill structures probably protect and aid the birds in prying up mollusks and similar prey.

The American, or common, eider has a circumpolar distribution and on this continent ranges from above Hudson Bay to New England and occasionally farther south. The drake is a large, heavy-bodied black and white duck with a green patch on the rear of the head. At a distance, the bird looks white above, black below. The king eider is another circumpolar species. Its North American populations migrate from the far north down through Alaska and western Canada to Oregon, and down through the Great Lakes as well as the Atlantic Coast to New

The northern eider is an Arctic species which hunters in the United States seldom see.

York—and occasionally to the Carolinas. It has a gray head with green cheek patches, black wings, and a mostly black body with a white neck, breast, and flank patches. The wings have white covert patches and pale undersides. Both American and king eider hens have drab brownish coloration.

The American, or common, scoter is another far northern breeder that winters along both coasts—down to Puget Sound in the West and the Carolinas in the East. The drake is our only duck with entirely black plumage. Nevertheless, it looks much like our other scoters in flight because they are all so dark. Where one is legal game, all scoters are legal. The hen is dark brown, appearing black at a distance.

The surf scoter comes down from the Arctic and subarctic along the West Coast to Mexico, through Canada to the Great Lakes, and down the East Coast to the Carolinas. One of its nicknames, skunkhead, refers to two oblong white patches over its forehead and nape. The remainder of its plumage is black. The hen is brownish with mottled gray underparts.

The white-winged scoter nests from the Arctic down to the north-central states and winters down to Baja California and the Carolinas, with a few joining the surf scoters on the Great Lakes. Both sexes have a white speculum; the drake is mostly black, the hen dark brown, and both sexes look black at a distance.

In some coastal locales—particularly upper New England—gunning for sea ducks is a tradition. Mostly scoters are taken, but a few eiders are bagged, too. Some of the shooting is done from small, rocky coastal islands and some is done from boats, even in a choppy sea. Lines of simple black floating jugs or blocks are strung out to decoy the flights, which tend to come in very low, sometimes just above the waves, when the wind rises and visibility is limited. There are times when shooting is tricky from a rolling boat, and rough weather often makes this specialized sport very exciting, even dangerous. It can also be plain cold, wet, and miserable.

Scoters are often called coot, though they are unrelated to the American coot, which is an aquatic bird but not a true duck.

CHAPTER 4

GEESE AND BRANT

The 1990s may well be the most crucial period in the history of waterfowl conservation. A combination of recent wildlife calamities (chiefly due to climatic conditions and habitat shrinkage) and new game-management programs has produced a spate of reports in all the media—some of them unjustifiably pessimistic. Despite enormous continuing problems, there is no reason to believe the doomsday stories, especially those about wild geese.

The truth is that few outdoor sports today have such a promising future as goose hunting. There was a time when only a few lucky sportsmen could hunt these magnificent game birds, but now anyone can experience the exhilaration of this superlative form of waterfowling. And in spite of periodic ups and downs in waterfowl numbers, there are signs that the situation over the long term will continue to improve with regard to geese.

To estimate populations, ground and air surveys are conducted during the nesting season by state and provincial agencies, the Canadian government, the U.S. Fish and Wildlife Service, and Ducks Unlimited. For many years, *Sports Afield* and other magainzes have published annual reports of these surveys, and the news releases issued by Ducks Unlimited carry frequent reports. In 1987, *Sports Afield*'s "Waterfowl Forecast" described a nesting season only a little better than the previous year's for ducks, but noted that "geese, particularly Canada geese, continue to produce record numbers throughout their ranges, except in the Arctic, where a late thaw allowed little, if any, reproduction."

Even in the Arctic there was some good news: Alaska's emperor geese showed a 23 percent increase that same season. Moreover, some of our most advanced management techniques are more effective with geese than with most ducks. For example, geese can be more easily induced to nest in new areas. The long-term outlook is therefore good, and in many regions sportsmen are being encouraged to spend more days hunting geese rather than ducks.

Two species of brant—which are small geese—provide sport and fine eating on the East and West Coast. Apart from these, North America has four varieties of geese that are of major interest to sportsmen: the Canada, the snow, the blue, and the white-fronted (or specklebelly) goose. The blue is a color phase of the snow goose rather than a separate species, but is encountered only in certain regions and is therefore considered a distinct variety. Two other species, the emperor goose and Ross's goose, are encountered in limited regions.

Canada Goose

The designation Canada goose covers several closely related subspecies that vary mostly in size, from the three-and-a-half-pound-average Richardson's goose through the cackling goose, the lesser Canada and the common Canada, which averages eight or nine pounds. There is also a giant Canada subspecies which averages about sixteen pounds. This gargantuan goose was thought to be extinct until a wintering flock was discovered near Rochester, Minnesota, in

The gander standing on shore is a Canada. The odd-looking bird in the water is a hybrid Canada/emperor goose. The locale is Lakeview, Oregon, far south of the emperor's normal range, although a few of these birds winter from Washington to California. (*Edward P. Cliff, U.S. Forest Service*)

1962. Since then, a few flocks have been established elsewhere, and the giant Canadas have extended their range, sometimes mingling with smaller relatives. A mature eastern Canada goose is apt to weigh no more than seven or possibly eight pounds, yet hunters occasionally bag one weighing ten or more. This may indicate a few instances of hybridizing with the giant race. Except for size, all of the Canada geese look pretty much the same, with black necks and white cheeks.

The common Canada goose, or honker, is surely one of the most magnificent birds in the world. Whether resting on water or grazing on land, these brownish-gray geese with long black necks held straight upright are easy to recognize. The white cheek patches and the clearly defined base of the black stocking are charac-

teristic and easy to notice. Honkers swim gracefully in the manner of swans and they can swim rapidly if necessary. Considering their size and structure, they are also very agile on land.

During flight, the large gray bodies and long black necks of Canada geese are also unmistakable. On short flights they may travel in small groups and give the impression that their flying is labored. But during high-altitude or migration travel, their flight seems extremely graceful. During these migrations the geese fly in the familiar undulating V-shaped formations which sometimes change to a long single line or Indian file. Rising from land or water, geese ordinarily take several steps to gain takeoff. When suddenly surprised, they can spring into the air with a single bound.

The wariness and intelligence of Canadian

A goose hunter in the rice fields near Eagle Lake, Texas, where snows, blues, and white-fronts are the most abundant game. The makeshift but effective decoys in this photo are large pieces of white cardboard, and note that the hunter is totally clad in white.

Surrounded by stickup honker decoys, these hunters are gunning from a roomy four-man pit blind in a stubble field. The hunter at far left is the well-known writer Gene Hill. A renowned shotgunner, Gene owns several of the latest-model guns but in this picture he's using a very old favorite—an ancient Winchester Model 97 pump. (*Steve Ferber*)

Canada geese rising from their resting waters to head for nearby feeding fields in Union County, Illinois. (*Illinois Department of Conservation*)

Perhaps the greatest sight in a goose hunter's world is when Canadas set their wings, as here, to descend toward decoys.

honkers is as well known as their characteristic honking cry. Whenever feeding, either on land or water, it always seems that at least part of the flock is on the alert for approaching danger. A warning from any one of the birds, and all necks suddenly raise and in the next instant the flock is airborne. They have very keen eyesight and their hearing is remarkable.

The various kinds of Canadas nest almost completely across Canada and in portions of the northwestern United States and into Alaska. In several states in the eastern half of the United States, local goose flocks have been established or are in the process of being established. The basis or core of such a process is a large lake or marsh that becomes a refuge. Here a flock of geese can rest or loiter and never be disturbed.

The Canada goose flock is established in various ways, at first by feeding or baiting heavily to arrest wild birds during migration and later by encouraging them to nest, thereby building a native flock. These wild geese tend to nest in the places where they learn to fly, and an increasing number of birds return to the local refuges each fall. This scheme supplements the production of geese in the far north with birds reared at points throughout the country.

Canada goose flocks have been established at many sites, including Missouri's Swan Lake Wild Life Refuge and the adjacent Fountain

When shooting from a pit in a stubble field, a hunter can place a few of his honker decoys right next to the blind and can cover the pit roof with cornstalks, thus adding to the deception. (*Will Ryan*)

A typical goose blind in the East—in this case at Lake Mattamuskeet. (*State of North Carolina Photo, Bill Gulley*)

The author, draped in a white bed sheet, holds up a rice-field snow goose. The variable-choke device on the muzzle of Bauer's gun is the old-style Cutts type.

Grove State Wildlife area; in Minnesota at Red Lake, Agassiz, and Tamarack National Wildlife Refuges; in Illinois, at Horseshoe Lake, Union County, and Crab Orchard; in Nebraska at Crescent Lake; in North Dakota at Upper and Lower Souris; in South Dakota at Lacreek, Sand Lake, and Waubay; in Wisconsin at Necedah and Horicon Marsh; in Michigan at Seney and Shiawassee National Wildlife Refuges; in Tennessee at Chickamauga Lake; in South Carolina at the Santee Cooper System; in Maryland in Kent County; in Ontario at Jack Miner Sanctuary; in Kentucky in Ballard County; in Ohio at Lake Saint Marys, Mosquito Reservoir, and O'Shaughnessy Reservoir; in Pennsylvania at

Pymatuning Reservior; in Indiana at Hovey Lake.

Of course, there are many other goose concentrations besides these, especially in the West, where it hasn't been necessary to build captive or artificial flocks. A list of these places would be almost impossible to compile, but a good example is the Missouri River bottomland area south of Helena, Montana. Another is the Arkansas River bottoms of Colorado.

A hunter's best bet is to contact his state conservation department for information on these goose areas. In some cases the hunt as well as the flocks are controlled. Hunting at many is permitted on an allotment or lottery basis and sometimes there is a nominal fee for blinds and transportation to them.

Snow Goose and Blue Goose

Two races of snow geese, greater and lesser, are native to North America. Both nest in the extreme Canadian north and both are favorites with sportsmen. Completely snow-white of plumage except for black wingtips, the snow goose is called ghost goose by the Cree Indians and in a few regions is also known as wa-wa (an Indian name for wild goose). In the southern states it is sometimes called a white brant.

The greater snow goose averages six or seven pounds; the lesser averages about five. Ross's goose, a close relative but classified as a separate species, generally weighs only about two and a half pounds—a mallard-sized goose. Lesser snows winter chiefly in central California and along the Louisiana and Texas Gulf Coast. In recent years, however, they have extended their range eastward, undoubtedly mingling and sometimes perhaps breeding with the greater snows that winter along the Atlantic Coast, chiefly from Virginia into the Carolinas.

For many years, snow geese could not be hunted along the Atlantic Flyway. At the time of this writing, they are legal game and abundant. No doubt their numbers have multiplied partly as a result of full protection and good habitat conditions (both for breeding and wintering) during a number of successive seasons. But the increase may also be due in part to an influx of lesser snows.

Ross's goose concentrates its wintering in

A blue goose in Texas. (*N. Kent, U.S. Fish & Wildlife Service*)

central California, where lesser snows also gather, but the two have somewhat different breeding areas and there is no evidence that hybridization occurs, except perhaps very infrequently.

Differentiating between two races of snow geese can be impossible, but snows are easy to tell from other waterfowl. Our only other waterfowl with all-white plumage are swans, which have much longer necks, slower wingbeats, and no black at the wingtips.

Except for very young birds at the beginning of the season, snows tend to be wary. Paradoxically, they sometimes descend in great and determined numbers on preferred feeding sites such as southern rice fields. Hunters may encourage them with white shell and/or windsock decoys—or quite often simply by scattering a great many white rags about a field. When clad in white coveralls, the gunners themselves seem to function as giant decoys. At the height of the season and with the right weather, the normally shy birds may amply demonstrate the origin of the expression, "silly as a goose."

Both lesser and greater snows generally fly high and fast in long, diagonal lines or in V flocks, usually calling shrilly as they go. Their cries, higher pitched than those of Canada geese, are sometimes described as yelping. On the West Coast, if a flock of white geese passes silently overhead, you can assume they're Ross's geese even if you can't be certain of their size because Ross's geese seldom call while in flight.

For many years, game biologists and ornithologists disputed whether the blue goose should be classified as a separate species or sub-species or merely a color phase (genetic color variation) of the lesser snow goose. Scientists have now determined that the blue is, indeed, just a color phase, but the bird is so distinctive in its coloration and range that a great many sportsmen will always regard it as a separate variety.

Blues nest chiefly on the tundra of Baffin Island and adjacent lands in extreme northern Canada. Although their breeding range overlaps that of lesser snows only on the western periphery, interbreeding is common between the two color phases.

Blues begin heading south in the first weeks of September, but they dally along the way, particularly on the shores of Hudson Bay and the salt marshes of James Bay, where goose shooting is superlative when the season first opens. Outfitters fly hundreds of sportsmen up to the James Bay area each year, and Cree guides put out goose-wing decoys on the golden grasslands. Crees seldom if ever blow mechanical goose calls, but with their mouths and cupped hands can imitate a snow or blue—or a Canada, for that matter—to perfection.

Excellent gunning for blues is not confined to Canada. In late October, flights of blues, some of them traveling in their own flocks and some in mixed flocks with snows, head down the Mississippi Flyway. They are bagged in a number of states, of course, but by far the greatest concentrations winter on the Gulf Coast of Louisiana. They also come in splendid numbers to

Snow geese. (*Karl H. Maslowski*)

A lesser snow goose at a Texas wintering area. (*W. F. Kubichek, U.S. Fish & Wildlife Service*)

Hunting snows and blues near Fort Albany on the west shore of James Bay, Ontario. Perhaps this is the greatest goose shooting in America.

the rice fields of Texas and the coast of Mississippi, and have been extending their range to the east and north.

Like the snow goose, the blue has a pink or reddish bill with a white nail and black "grinning patch," and its head and neck are white. However, its body is mostly grayish-brown. Its common name is derived primarily from the wings, which seem to have a bluish tone when viewed from a distance. Many hunters swear they can discern no blue whatever, but the bird is easily identified since we have no other dark-bodied goose with an entirely white head and neck.

Blues usually fly in uneven or broken mixtures of V's and irregular lines, or mixed in with a flight of snows. In flight they constantly call, uttering a high-pitched *goop, goop* that can easily be distinguished from the honking of Canada geese. Interestingly, blues will come to all-white decoys just as eagerly as snows, and both blues and snows will often approach for a close look at a darker spread of Canada-goose decoys.

Emperor Goose

This is the least familiar of all American geese, because it never leaves Alaska. Known

widely among Alaskans as the Eskimo or painted goose, it nests in the coastal areas along the Bering Sea and its migration to wintering areas is only a short hop to points along the Alaskan Peninsula and the Aleutian Islands. The emperor is a handsome, medium-size bird. On the water in good sunlight its body may appear silvery gray. It resembles the blue goose except for the black marking on the underside of the neck. This same black neck marking is its best identification during flight.

The voice of the emperor goose is shrill and unqiue. During flight it constantly calls a shrill *klaha, klaha, klaha,* and when feeding it uses a great variety of conversational grunts and other sounds.

Emperor geese average about six or six and a half pounds in weight. There is great disagreement as to their quality as table birds, although Eskimos along the western Alaskan coast depend upon them for food and for feathers.

American Brant

The American brant is a small, handsome goose not much larger than a mallard or a canvasback duck. It is truly a sea goose, since it is seldom found very far from salt water. It is an extremely graceful, swift-flying bird. On the water it sits as high and lightly as a gull, with tail upraised and head poised. In the air it can flash downwind past a blind before a hunter has time to flip the safety of his gun.

American brant nest as far north in Canada as any other game birds. There is also a nesting colony along the northwest shore of Greenland. All of their wintering is confined to the Atlantic Coast, from Connecticut to North Carolina, an area where a chief food, eel grass, grows extensively in shallow bays and estuaries. Unlike geese, these brant seldom feed on land but rather follow the ebbing tide to find the food

American brant on Delaware Bay. These birds have paler underparts than the black brant of the Pacific Coast, but the two varieties are quite similar.

they need. They rarely dive for food but feed by tipping, as do the puddle ducks.

Most sportsmen who know them agree that the American brant is one of the finest game birds of all on the table. The meat is consistently tender and mild in flavor. In the old days of market hunting, brant often commanded the highest prices of any waterfowl.

On the water or in flight the brant appears as a black goose with whitish or gray sides. It looks very much like its first cousin, the black brant of the Pacific, but its sides do not show as much white as the Pacific bird. American brant fly in long, wavy, undulating lines and sometimes in regular V-formations. Their voices, which are loud and metallic, can often be heard a long distance away. A juvenile black brant has an all-black neck, but mature birds have thin white slashes or a broken white stripe on each side of the black neck.

They feed most actively—seeking eel grass in the shallows—when the tide is at half flood or half ebb. They are normally wary, but when seeking food they come to decoys eagerly.

Black Brant

The black brant, which is very similar in appearance and habits to the American brant, is confined to the Pacific Coast. It nests along the north shore of Alaska and eastward toward the Mackenzie Delta of Canada. It winters along our Pacific Coast from Puget Sound southward through Baja California. In the latter place I have found it abundant along sand beaches, where fast evening shooting is possible as late as March.

The bird has darker underparts than its Atlantic cousin and larger, more distinct white markings—almost a collar—on its neck. There can be no confusion, since the two varieties are separated by a continent. The flight of the black brant is fast, as the bird moves with rapid wing strokes and often travels very close to the water in an undulating flight path. It frequently changes elevation, probably moving up and down with wind currents. During flight it utters a low guttural sound that almost resembles a

A Cree hunting guide at work in Ontario. The hunters have bagged several geese, and the guide is propping them up as effective additions to the decoy spread.

growling. Like the American brant, it is delicious on the table.

White-Fronted Goose

The white-fronted, or specklebelly, goose is a bird that only western and southern gunners are likely to see. It nests in northern Alaska and extreme northwestern Canada and winters along the Texas and Louisiana Gulf Coast, in northwestern Mexico, and in central California. It is a very handsome and striking bird, very good on the table, but probably the least sophisticated of all our native geese. On a number of occasions I have seen this species fly within easy range of gunners who were standing in the open. Often it travels in the company of blue and snow geese.

This bird can be identified on the water because it is the only goose with brown head, chest, neck, and underparts. The white front for which it is named isn't always conspicuous. It's only a white facial patch around the bill. The speckled or checkered belly is more visible. If not too far away, the barred, blotched, or speckled dark-and-white breast is a good mark of identification during flight. During migration they fly high in V-shaped flocks and therefore somewhat resemble Canada geese. Their call in flight is a cackle, which some gunners have described as laughter.

Most geese nest in the north, chiefly in Canada, and winter in the United States. But under normal conditions they also make daily migrations; two round trips, morning and evening, from resting grounds or refuge areas to feeding areas. The feeding areas may be on land or water, but most likely are on land because geese are grazers. Hunting them is generally planned to take advantage of these daily migrations.

There are a number of ways to hunt geese. For instance, when they are loitering along a river it is possible to camouflage a canoe or shallow-draft skiff to resemble a pile of debris and to drift downstream into shooting range. This method, often called floating, is described as duck "freelancing" in another chapter, but for geese it is a pretty chancy method. So is stalking them on foot.

Geese on the ground, except in long-established refuges, are extremely wary. Stalking them successfully is usually a slow and tedious process during which a sportsman must take every advantage of cover and terrain. But usually there is little cover and nine times in ten the stalker must crawl face down on either a frozen turf or through gumbo mud. The object, of course, is to get within range before flushing, or "jumping," the birds, and the technique is known as jump-shooting.

Flyway shooting is by far the deadliest technique. First you locate your flock of geese, then observe its flight route between resting and feeding areas. It is along this route that a man finds his shooting.

But how do you find resting and feeding grounds? Sometimes with field glasses. Other times you may have to follow the flying birds, at a distance naturally, in a car across the countryside. It's a good idea to ask farmers and rural mail carriers to keep you posted on feeding flights.

When you have located a feeding area, you are ready to go hunting. If the geese have not been molested on an evening flight, they will probably follow the same route the next morning, and vice versa. Your next step is to find a good interception point somewhere along the flight route. You dig a pit or build a blind, put out a spread of decoys, and wait hopefully. But it may be a long, uncomfortable wait.

Whereas smaller waterfowl begin to move at daybreak and even before dawn regardless of weather, geese are much more leisurely. If the weather is bad they may not begin to fly until midmorning. A homeward evening flight may start in midafternoon. Occasionally geese may be coming and going at the same time, with the flight continuing all day long. At such times a clever hunter can station himself so as to enjoy good pass-shooting.

The term "pass-shooting" is so universally and loosely used that it requires an explanation. Quite often it means shooting at geese or ducks that happen to be flying within range over your blind while traveling to or from feeding or resting areas, as opposed to shooting over decoys.

However, there are times when your blind may be situated in a veritable sea of decoys and you will be pass-shooting all the same. This generally occurs when your blind is on a local flyway—between resting and feeding sites, pref-

A Maryland hunter with big honkers bagged from a cornfield blind.

erably nearer to one of these sites than the other so that the birds are not crossing at peak altitude.

Sure, they may approach your decoys or be lured closer by calling, but they may only pass high over your blind—but in range if you're a good enough wingshot. They may have been feeding or resting at one site for days or nights on end, and nothing will deter them from reaching their destination. Or, from the air, they may see birds of their kind feeding or resting in the distance—in greater numbers and more alluring than your decoys. Regardless of your decoying and calling, they may merely pass you, and that, too, provides an opportunity for pass-shooting.

The flight-interception strategy will work anywhere in America, with regional variations. In Texas, for example, the blues fly to rice fields to feed, in Maryland the Canadas look for corn-fields, and in the Dakotas you'll find geese in wheat stubble. Differences in blinds and decoys vary geographically, too.

Somebody once said geese can be the dumbest and wisest of all birds, and there is evidence to support this comment. For instance, they often show great gullibility about decoys. On a hunt at Eagle Lake, Texas, I was amazed to find that my guide carried several dozen white "Tom McCready for Sheriff" placards to be used as decoys. He folded each just once and scattered them at random around a pit blind.

"We look more like litterbugs," I commented, "than goose hunters."

"Baby diapers work just as well," he answered, "but after the election these are free."

The placards worked unbelievably well. We bagged six mixed geese, the legal limit at the time, and then settled back to watch the mar-

Sunset on a Canada goose resting area in Maryland.

velous spectacle of geese winging everywhere on the horizon.

Expert goose hunters are divided on the matter of calls, but almost all depend on one to supplement their decoys. Calling, however, is such a vast and complicated subject that it can't be tackled here. The beginner would do well to let a guide or experienced hand do the calling. Or he might visit a refuge and try to imitate what he hears there.

Another alternative is to buy an instructional cassette. The better tapes feature a master caller who provides verbal instructions and explanations interspersed with demonstrations of various calls typifying a given species. The Can-

ada goose, for example, utters a surprising number of vocalizations, and the differences between them can be subtle. A few tapes also come with printed instructions. Pay close attention to the instructions or you may inadvertently flare the geese just before they come within range by emitting an alarm call when you mean to entice them with a gathering call. Practice imitating what you hear on the tape and, if you're like most gunners, you will soon find that realistic goose calling is considerably easier than calling ducks effectively.

Goose hunting is a great sport any way you look at it, but it is never more exciting than the day you yourself call a goose into shotgun range.

CHAPTER 5

MYSTERY BIRDS OF THE MARSHES

It may sound strange to sportsmen elsewhere across the land, but some of America's most traditional hunting depends on a high tide along the Atlantic Seaboard. It begins in September, as it has since Colonial times, when tides flood the estuaries, the river mouths, and the saltwater flats from New England to the Carolinas. It's then and there that clapper rails— the "railbirds" of the Jersey shore and the "marsh hens" of Chesapeake Bay—are most abundant and therefore ready for autumn's harvest.

Classic railbirding has changed very little since the first generation of rail hunters set the pattern. Today, as always, it's a two-man team affair: one man to stand and shoot; another to pole a double-ended boat through the flooded marsh grasses. Even the boat's design is little altered since those early days. One old reference described a railbirding boat like this: "Square ends front and back, with a draft shallow enough to follow a mule as it sweats up a dusty road." Craft that closely fit these specifications are standard to this day on the Connecticut, the Choptank, and on other rivers in clapper country.

Even though rail hunting has persisted along the seaboard, it never really caught on in mid-America, where other species of rails are actually more plentiful than clappers are along the coast. It seems incredible in these times of limited game bags that game birds by the millions can funnel down our flyways every autumn and be almost completely ignored by American hunters. But it's true. Seasons on them are long (up to seventy days), bag limits are liberal, and there are splendid gunning possibilities in nearly every state.

During the peaks of migrations rails swarm in swamps and marshlands in every state of the Union.

Six kinds of rails (soras, kings, Virginias, clappers, and the rarely killed black rails and yellow rails) and two kinds of gallinules (Floridas and purples) comprise an underharvested resource. At least one of these species is native in every corner of the land. Several pass through most of our shallow wetlands en route from nesting grounds in the north (often in the far north) to wintering areas in the Caribbean or points still farther south.

Sora Rail

The soras, or Carolina rails, are the most abundant of all. They're the most widely distributed because they nest in bogs and marshes everywhere across the northern United States and all through Canada. They're prolific breeders and during a fall migration will suddenly descend on marshy areas in astonishing numbers. Just as suddenly, almost, when the temperature falls or when there is a heavy frost, they disappar again, headed farther south. Nowadays when anyone mentions rail shooting in mid-America, he's usually speaking of soras.

Averaging eight or nine inches long and weighing about half as much as an average bob-white, soras are brownish in color and have chickenlike beaks. They become restless at the first signs of autumn. Evidently they gather in

A hunter pushes through heavy cattail cover, flushes a sora rail, and then holds up several soras. It's tough going in boggy cover, but the shooting is fairly easy.

flights and travel at night, for one morning a previously barren marsh will be full of them. The main flights in the northern United States begin around September 1, and generally they have passed into the wintering areas in the West Indies and elsewhere by the end of October.

Soras are not fast, strong flyers. They do not rise far above the marsh grasses when flushed, and they have a habit of circling. To a beginner at rail hunting it's a tricky maneuver, but eventually the birds become easy targets. After fattening on the succulent seeds of the swamps through late summer, they're extremely delicious on the table.

King Rail and Virginia Rail

Largest of American rails is the king. It's a handsome bird with a long bill, dark-brown back, and cinnamon-colored breast, and is thin enough to have inspired the expression "skinny as a rail." Except in certain times and places, kings never approach the abundance of soras, but like soras, they're splendid fare on the table. A king will average about seventeen inches in length and will have a two-foot wingspread.

The range of the king is smaller than the so-

A king rail feeding amid typical vegetation at the Sabine National Wildlife Refuge in Louisiana.
(*Julian Howard, U.S. Fish & Wildlife Service*)

ra's. It is concentrated in the freshwater marshes of the Eastern United States, but is sometimes found west to Minnesota. It is less secretive, a more powerful flyer, and consequently a harder-to-hit target.

Between the king and the sora, both in size and abundancee, is the Virginia rail. In appearance it is practically a pocket edition of the king. It is almost continent-wide in distribution, and prefers freshwater bogs and wetlands.

Clapper Rail

In Atlantic saltwater areas, the best-known rail hunting is for the clappers. The bird is darker and slightly smaller than the king, and its range is limited to the East and West Coasts. Despite food habits which tend to animals (fiddlers, shrimp, crabs, mollusks, insects) rather than vegetable materials, it is also a highly regarded table bird. The clapper's flight is probably the strongest of all rails, but still the bird is an easier target than ducks or geese.

Rail hunting can be extremely difficult or extremely easy, depending mostly on water levels. Generally the freshwater rails prefer the shallowest areas, and so it's necessary to hunt them on foot. Since the cover is invariably dense and the going slow, as in any marsh, hunting can get to be a rugged business. It is not always easy to flush the birds, either, because kings and so-

Hunting clapper rails along the tidal marshes of the Atlantic Coast. A light punt boat is commonly used to get through grassy areas. (*D. N. Deane, Connecticut State Board of Fisheries*)

Most rail shooting is warm-weather sport, as the season opens early. There are still a few professional "pushers"—guides who pole the boat and are thoroughly at home on the tidal marshes. Shown here are a pusher and his client. Some gunners go out in pairs so they can take turns pushing and gunning.

ras can more easily escape by running through or under the marsh grass than by flying over it—so in most cases a close-working dog is a valuable asset.

Pointing dogs have little value in rail hunting. I've seen springer spaniels that worked well ahead of a gunner, and retrievers such as Labradors and goldens are the best of all, to retrieve game as well as to flush it. A winged or crippled bird nearly always escapes without a dog because of the nature of the cover and because the bird can swim or dive.

One reason rail hunting isn't as popular as it might be is the uncertainty of their flights. At least, hunters aren't always able to find the birds. Actually it isn't too difficult, for there are a number of ways to discover with reasonable accuracy when and where the birds will enter any locality.

Local open seasons partially pinpoint the peaks of rail and gallinule flights. These seasons begin early everywhere and they're calculated to be open during the main flight in any region. Opening day, for example, is set to allow for a very early flight, and closing day (usually more than two months later) for an extremely late flight. The main flight is figured to arrive during the middle of the season. All rails are very sensitive to falling temperatures and frosts. These can start moving the birds southward. It's a wise sportsman who watches for noticeable weather changes just to the north of him. Every state conservation department has a migratory-bird or waterfowl biologist who knows better than most when flights occur or are expected. Local bird-watchers and ornithologists also keep pretty close track of these movements, and are accurate sources of information. But the most positive method is to make a personal reconnaissance. You'll also learn plenty about other marsh critters—about the ducks and geese—for hunting seasons later on.

Rail-Hunting Methods

Occasionally special situations—such as the rice or millet harvest in the lower Mississippi Valley—will concentrate the birds enough to make hunting on foot a relatively leisurely pastime, but usually it's a matter of slogging through cattails, smartweed, and the like to put birds in the air. Try to concentrate on areas of vegetation heavy with seeds. This is rough going when the weather is warm, but it will put game in the bag and your legs in shape for upland seasons later on.

Concentrate on the edges of marshes. Usually the weeds here grow especially lush, and it's no picnic to wade through them. But it's precisely here that the most rails will be. Never pass up the small islands or fingers of land in marshes, or the weedy edges of dikes, fills, and embankments. The upper, shallow sections of reservoirs and headwater lakes are always favorite stopovers for rails, especially for soras; so are the swampy flats created by beaver workings. Farm ponds sometimes attract them. Obviously, several hunters can be more successful by walking abreast quickly through such cover

The common, or Florida, gallinule is an underharvested bird in some regions. Although seasons and bag limits tend to be liberal, very few gunners go hunting specifically for this bird. (*Karl H. Maslowski*)

because the birds can elude a single hunter more easily.

Veterans of marsh-hen hunting use a couple of tricks that save plenty of steps in a season of hunting. First they listen for the birds to spot concentrations of them. Rails give a harsh, somewhat strident *yick, yick, yick* call that is usually answered by other rails. Of course, it's a dead giveaway to their location once a hunter learns to identify the call. It takes some experience, though, because many similar sounds are common to a marsh.

Another old trick is to circle and test suitable cover by tossing sticks or clods of earth into it. When something falls nearby, a rail will usually call in alarm, and again other rails will answer.

Since the best rail hunting occurs in warm weather and over wet ground, it's best to dress lightly. It's hard to beat a cotton khaki shirt and trousers. Most hunters prefer to tramp the marshes "wet"—with cotton socks and tennis shoes—but nowadays there are plenty of extra-lightweight waders on the market. The best shooting is early in the morning, for several reasons. It's cooler, the rails are more active, they call more frequently, and the entire marsh is more "alive" at this time.

The most ideal conditions exist on a high tide, when it's possible to hunt rails from a boat—as along the Atlantic Coast. Of course, it's also possible in freshwater marshes crisscrossed with channels or other waterways. Here it can actually be a leisurely, almost lazy, sport for the gunner. Any canoe or shallow-draft boat might be used, but the best craft is the old punt boat used by generations of eastern clapper hunters. Great Lakes duckboats, similar in construction, also do the job. In both of these, the gunner sits or stands in the bow while the boatman poles the boat from the stern.

Seaboard sportsmen keep a weather eye for a high tide combined with a steady onshore wind. This combination floods vast areas of marsh seldom covered otherwise, and it permits a boat to weave in and out of patches of vegetation, flushing birds that are concentrated in a smaller area. Where the vegetation is most dense, the boatman uses his push-pole to "pat the lettuce," to flush birds as much as to move the boat. It all amounts to splendid sport, for a rail swinging with a brisk wind becomes a difficult target.

A good many rails come to bag when hunters work the sloughs and channels of freshwater wetlands. Sometimes it's possible to mix boat hunting with walking, or to hunt from a boat while a retriever beats the heavy cover on the bank. Occasionally it's even possible to find these birds in numbers on bare mud flats. Rail hunting has endless possibilities for a sportsman who wants a full calendar afield.

The best scattergun for marsh-hen shooting is the 20 gauge with light loads. The birds are fragile, they rarely flush at long range, and it doesn't take a heavy load to collect them. The only gun once permitted in an old rail-shooting club on the New Jersey coast was a single-shot .410. Be sure to check your state's regulations. You'll almost surely be required to use steel shot, which rules out the .410. With steel, you'll want the smallest available pellet size.

Besides a day in the field during the most elegant time of year, this hunting offers one more bonus to American sportsmen—distinctively delicious meat for the table. Here's a recipe to try:

Broiled Rail. Peel the birds by removing the heads, slitting down the backs and completely skinning them. Cut off the breast portion and discard the rest. Prepare a liquor of vinegar and melted butter in which a kernel of garlic has been finely ground. Baste the breasts liberally using the sauce and place them over a small bed of charcoal. Be careful not to place them too close to the heat. Turn the birds often for five or six minutes, depending on their size, and baste each time. Served with cornbread and a green salad, they're the finest recommendation for marsh-hen hunting anyone can offer.

Coot and Gallinule

Occasionally, hunters seeking rails (or ducks, for that matter) may also bag gallinules and/or common coot. The coot is a black, webless water bird with lobed toes to aid it in swimming. It rarely ventures more than a few feet onto land. This bird takes off from the water rather awkwardly and does not fly as fast as most ducks, but it provides good wingshooting practice, is tasty when prepared properly, and is plentiful in a great many regions.

Gallinules are seldom as plentiful as rails, but they're also available during long seasons and

The jacksnipe, abundant in many areas, is a really great game bird. (*Karl H. Maslowski*)

they are probably better flyers. Two species—Floridas, also known as common gallinules, which are plentiful and distributed almost nationwide, and purples, which are restricted to the South—frequent approximately the same cover as rails. They prefer a little more water with their weeds, though, and they swim more often and more expertly than rails.

Snipe

For every serious sportsman, there are certain days afield more memorable than all the rest. One of mine occurred early in October on the Albany River delta in far northern Ontario.

Lou Klewer and I were hunting geese on a morning when blue geese flew so fast and furiously that we needed less than an hour to bag a couple of limits. But that isn't my story. While Willie Wesley, our Cree caller, collected the decoys and the dead geese, Lou and I strolled out across the grassy tundra, which now seemed like liquid, flowing gold in the Arctic wind. We hadn't walked very far before we found the grass was full of jacksnipe. They flushed ahead of us and from almost underfoot in unbelievable numbers.

"I never saw so many . . ." Lou began.

"Let's go back and get the guns," I interrupted.

It's possible we set a new record for the quar-

Hunting snipe on wide, wet short-grass flats—where shots are seldom as close as this. (*Charles F. Waterman*)

ter mile, at least on a soggy track, back to our goose blind. Then with pockets full of shells we started walking again.

A few old-time hunters will know what happened next. We enjoyed the kind of steady shooting which doesn't exist anymore except in lonely, out-of-the-way places like that one. We had shots at singles and we had shots at doubles. We even had covey shots. Birds flushed ahead of us and they flushed behind. That cover was simply loaded with snipe and they boiled up and out of it at every conceivable angle. Some would fly low, barely skimming the tips of waving grass, but others would zoom upward, catch a gust of wind and then disappear a mile a minute toward the horizon.

Until I settled down, my shooting was a study in futility. I missed seven straight snipe before I finally tumbled a crossing shot. Then right away Lou scored a double and we began to do a little better. Still we had collected only a dozen birds before my shells—almost two boxes of them—finally ran out.

"I'm finished," I shouted to Lou, turning my pockets inside out.

"I still have two more," Lou answered, and then proceeded to miss the next two flushing snipe.

Let me say that it isn't customary for Lou to miss two consecutive shots at anything. But it's typical for jacksnipe to make monkeys of the best wingshots, because here is one of the greatest game birds on the face of the earth. For my money, the snipe is one of the toughest targets of all.

In camp that night, cleaning his side-by-side double with a silicone cloth, Lou said, "Let's skip the goose shooting in the morning and try those snipe instead."

He was practically reading my mind.

It wasn't long after daybreak before Lou and I were following a thin trail through the tall willows that sheltered our tent camp and bordered the Albany River in a few isolated places. A raw and icy wind whined in the treetops above us, and when we broke out into the open tundra, it was squarely in our faces. For a mile or more we fought the wind, shivering and hunting over the same ground that had been alive with snipe the day before. But now the cover was empty; we didn't flush a single bird. The hard ground and the crisp grass told the

A New England gunner with a brace of snipe. These birds offer a marvelous change of pace for hunters who want to come ashore or leave the blind for a while and stretch their legs. (*Dale C. Spartas*)

story. As soon as the tundra froze, the birds vanished into the night, no doubt to begin the first lap of the long migration southward.

The jacksnipe, Wilson's snipe, is surely one of the most interesting citizens of the world. Our American species is called Wilson's snipe because an ornithologist named Alexander Wilson first noticed that it was slightly different from the European snipe. But the differences are very minor.

Any jacksnipe is a widely traveled bird. The breeding range of the species includes the entire northern half of the United States, but no doubt most nesting is concentrated in Canada. The first freeze drives them south. Snipe feed by probing into the soft earth with long bills for worms and other edibles, and a frozen sod makes this impossible.

Snipe migrations are as unpredictable as the weather but it's safe to say that virtually all of

A pair of common coot. These birds are plentiful in many regions, and although they're not strong flyers they can offer good sport—and good shooting practice for waterfowlers. When properly prepared, they're tastier than most hunters realize.

them winter south of the frost line. One exception would include the occasional birds which are seen around the hot springs and geyser basins of Yellowstone Park during January. Nearly all prefer Florida and the Gulf states, the West Indies, Central America, and northern South America. I've had great success hunting them late in the year on the tide flats of Matanzas Bay below St. Augustine, Florida, and I have seen a few while hunting teal in Costa Rica.

An adult snipe is handsome or ungainly, depending on how you view the long bill and long legs. His back is a rich brown, his breast a lighter brown, and his belly white. He appears to be frail, and could be mistaken in flight for such shore birds as the yellowlegs, the plover, or even the dowitcher. None of these, however, has the same exciting, erratic flight so difficult to follow over a gun barrel.

Snipe seasons and limits, like those for rail, are generally liberal. Market shooting once accounted for a terrible toll, and the gradual destruction of habitat both on summering and wintering grounds caused the population to decline. Still there are quite a few snipe on the flyaways today, and the harvest by sportsmen is light.

There's one final word to be said about snipe: They are delicious on the table. Any recipe which is suitable for quail is also suitable here, but I have a favorite.

Snipe. Braise the whole birds in hot vegetable oil in a skillet. Now add salt, pepper, sour cream, and dry red wine, and cook them for no more than thirty minutes. Served with a green salad, cornbread, and cool ale, there's nothing—absolutely nothing—to match them on a happy autumn evening.

CHAPTER 6

BASIC DUCK AND GOOSE HUNTING

It was barely breaking day when Frank Sayers and I arrived at his Portage River marsh on a typical windy November morning. We parked his station wagon, shouldered a couple of sacks of decoys, and followed a trail to the shooting area atop a muddy dike. We were late this morning; ordinarily we would have been in the blind an hour before, but a flat tire had caused the delay.

Halfway to the shooting hole, Frank stopped short and dropped to his knees. I followed suit. Then by crawling forward on hands and knees, I saw what caused the sudden strange behavior. Maybe as many as a hundred mixed black ducks and baldpates were sitting on the marsh.

It was a cinch for a stalking job. We could crawl to point-blank range on the opposite side of the dike. Nothing to it at all.

"Let's try them," I whispered to Frank.

"No," Frank answered, "let's just chase them away!"

If you believe that a bird in the hand is worth two somewhere else, my friend's strategy will resemble madness. But Frank knew what he was doing when he walked nonchalantly on down the dike and watched the birds wing away. Thirty minutes later our decoys were on the water, the two of us were settled in the blind, and . . . in twos, threes, and small flocks the ducks began filtering back. They furnished consistent shooting and it wasn't long until we had collected limits and were picking up the decoys to go home.

Of course, it doesn't always work so perfectly, but Frank was playing the odds. If we had shot the birds on the flush, our best possible bag

would have been two birds each. That's good enough. But the rest of the ducks would have been spooked permanently.

Nine times in ten it's better to allow the birds to make an orderly escape. Whatever attracted them there in the first place will attract them again. If not unduly frightened, they will soon return. Of course, it's terribly hard to resist at times, but the wisest duck hunter is the man who makes it a rule never to shoot at large flocks of ducks, no matter how he encounters them.

As in any other kind of hunting, success is much a matter of knowing the critter you are hunting. If you understand ducks and the instincts which govern their movements, you can be a much better (and more interested) duck hunter. First let's examine the basic movements of North American ducks, because it's so important to understand these travels.

The Four Flyways

In 1935 government biologist Frederick Lincoln and his associates made a more thorough analysis than had ever been made before of the several thousand waterfowl band returns on hand. In other words, they assembled all the data available from previous banding of waterfowl and the returns of those bands, mostly by hunters. For example, if a bird was banded in Manitoba and its band was recovered by a hunter in South Carolina, they had some idea of the bird's travel. With thousands of such records on hand, it became apparent that North American waterfowl could be separated into

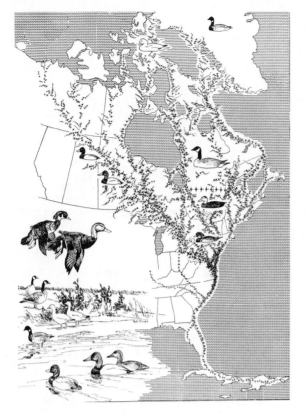

The Atlantic Flyway. (*U.S. Fish & Wildlife Service*)

The Mississippi Flyway. (*U.S. Fish & Wildlife Service*)

four separate flyways—known today as the Atlantic, Mississippi, Central, and Pacific Flyways. Waterfowl-hunting regulations are now formulated on a flyway basis. If one species becomes scarce in one flyway, shooting will be prohibited there, although it may be legal to hunt the species elsewhere.

Duck hunters and waterfowl biologists often use the terms flyway and migration routes. The term flyway can be used merely to describe a customary route used by birds between a resting and feeding area. But in the present context, a flyway is a vast geographic region with its own breeding area and wintering grounds. The two widely separated places are connected by a network of migration routes. In other words, a certain species will follow a certain migration route within its flyway when traveling from breeding to wintering areas in the fall. With only a few exceptions, they return north by the same routes in the springtime.

Each flyway has its own populations of waterfowl, even of species that are distributed completely across the continent or around the world. Of course, the breeding grounds of more than one flyway greatly overlap, and during the nesting season large areas are occupied by birds of the same species but of different flyways. The flyway maps in this chapter will illustrate this.

Many veteran waterfowlers will find it hard to believe, but the state of the weather has far less to do with the migrations of birds than is commonly believed. I have known old duck-hunting guides who felt they could predict the arrival of certain duck species by consulting a barometer and the long-range weather prediction. But any successful predictions are likely to be coincidental.

According to waterfowl biologists, migrations begin and end in obedience to physiological promptings governed by the shortening or lengthening of daylight hours. A migratory bird

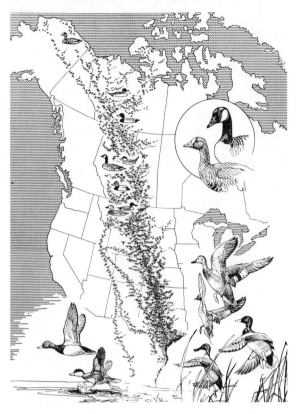

The Central Flyway. (*U.S. Fish & Wildlife Service*)

The Pacific Flyway. (*U.S. Fish & Wildlife Service*)

has what amounts to an internal (hormonal) clock and calendar. Of course, a severe storm or a sudden freeze may force ducks to move elsewhere, possibly farther south to survive. But annual migrations are a vital part of a wild duck's life cycle, and they have become adjusted to correspond with major seasonal changes.

The serious waterfowler can use a knowledge of migration routes and approximate dates to his own advantage. Let's assume he lives in Central City and hunts on the Central River sloughs. Every year, as accurately as possible, he keeps a chart on the arrival dates of fresh flights of mallards or pintails or whatever. Pretty soon he has an accurate record compiled over several seasons, and a quick glance will reveal at which periods the odds for shooting are most in his favor. He can better plan his trips and also make better use of the time he has available for hunting.

Hunting Tips for Early and Late Season

For many reasons, but mostly because the ducks are inexperienced and still unsophisticated, the shooting is best immediately after a "fresh" flight arrives from the north. But with continued hunting pressure, the ducks soon learn to avoid hunters and their devices. The more encounters with hunters, the more wary they become. Toward the end of the season, many ducks seem to know the brand names of all decoys.

There are good days to hunt ducks and there are poor ones. Every season is full of exceptions, but probably the best shooting occurs when the weather is worst—when a savage wind is howling out of the north or northeast and when the temperature is in the lower ranges. It may not

Gunning in a stretch of swampy "drowned timber," this duck hunter has strewn his boat with vegetation and is using it as a movable blind. (*Joe Richard*)

be a scientifically sound observation, but it seems to me that most species of ducks (scaup are notable exceptions) do not enjoy resting on very turbulent or choppy water. When the wind freshens, the ducks become increasingly restless and eventually fly out to look for more sheltered places to spend the day. In other words they will be circulating among inshore areas where hunting is possible. In addition, ducks fly lower on rainy or snowy days, evidently in order to get a clearer view of good places to land for resting or feeding.

Generally, the shooting is best very early and late in the day. This is because of the habit of flying from resting to feeding areas and back again at these two periods. I have enjoyed good shooting at high noon, but only rarely. It's better to spend middays elsewhere than in a cold blind. Take a nap, burn up some ammo on clay

pigeons, or make a reconnaissance to see where the ducks are resting.

A few sessions with clay targets can be great practice for any duck hunter, both before and during the open season. With a hand trap and a couple of cases of "birds," Frank Sayers and I toss all conceivable angles for each other to shoot. The crossing shots so common in duck hunting can be easily duplicated by tossing the clay targets directly across, in front of the shooter. Overhead shots, both from behind and from the front, can also be duplicated by standing behind and higher than the shooter or in defilade in front of him.

We've duplicated the high passing shots of ducks by tossing targets out the second-floor window of an old barn. We have also practiced shooting from a sitting position, a highly valuable drill if your plans include float-tripping for ducks by boat.

Preseason Reconnaissance

If you are a member of a duck club, most of your problems are solved. You simply make whatever reservations the club requires and then go shooting. The blinds, boats, decoys, and, you hope, the ducks are waiting. But if you don't belong to a club, your duck hunting should begin *before* opening day—except that you leave your gun at home. Take a road map and hiking shoes instead.

The first step is to locate the ducks, and the sooner the better. Find a migration route and then find specific places along the way where ducks are loitering. Next, try to determine their habits. See where they are feeding. Try to locate specifically the routes they fly between resting and feeding areas. Finally try to locate your blind (as long before opening day as logically possible) as conveniently as terrain, legal permission, and suitable water permit, to intercept the ducks somewhere or sometime during their daily routine. But keep in mind that once heavy gunning begins, their routine may be altered.

Owners' Permission

It is highly important to have clear-cut permission, preferably in writing (which is required by law in some states) before you

The view from a blind as a hunter tosses out decoys. This shows the relation between the blind's location and the placement of a decoy rig, or "stool."

Frank Sayers in a pit blind on a rocky Lake Erie island. When birds approach, he ducks down low.

trespass and build a blind. Laws are strange, vague, and varied in many states, especially as they pertain to riparian rights. Make certain you know them before blundering into legal trouble.

During preseason reconnaissance, carry good binoculars or a spotting scope. These optics are invaluable in locating resting flocks and flight lines, and will also save you making plenty of footprints across soggy real estate.

Talk to farmers when you can, or to the local game warden. He will know where waterfowl are concentrated. Sometimes rural mailmen are able to give tips on where they consistently see waterfowl during daily travels.

Public Hunting Areas

In all states there are public hunting areas that either were acquired especially for duck hunting or on which some duck hunting in season is possible. It's a good idea to inquire about these, and for that purpose a list of state conservation bureaus is furnished elsewhere in this volume. On many of these state lands, hunting is permitted for a low daily fee, for which a blind and boat are furnished. Where the demand for duck-hunting space is very great, the permits are issued on a lottery basis.

In some regions where waterfowling is an important activity, blinds or hunting areas can be rented by the day or leased for longer periods of time. Finding their locations is a matter of inquiring locally, or checking with the game warden or other conservation officials.

Safety

Those who have had little shooting or hunting experience will quickly discover that experienced gunners are extremely safety conscious. In fact, beginners usually learn how strictly they must observe safety rules before they ever have a chance to hunt, because most states now conduct a brief but thorough Hunter Safety Course which must be taken and passed before a person is allowed to buy a first hunting license. The establishment of the Hunter Safety Course has led to an enormously improved safety record throughout the country.

The rules that prevent accidents are a matter

This photo was taken from a natural blind—a streamside hiding spot on an Ohio river. Notice how ice has started to form around the edges. The hunter has just bagged two black ducks.

Crouching and moving ahead quietly, a puddle-duck hunter works his way along a drainage ditch. Farm-country ducks frequently loiter on waters as small as this, and they provide exciting jump-shooting.

A hunter waits in his blind on a small Midwestern farm pond. The blind can be makeshift or entirely natural, and very few decoys are needed to draw ducks to spots like this.

of common sense. For example, a shooter always assumes that a gun is loaded until he has opened the action of the firearm and checked both the magazine and the chamber for himself. For the same obvious reason, a shooter always points a gun in a safe direction—away from all other people who may be present—and never points it at anything he does not intend to shoot. No one with the slightest common sense climbs a fence or other obstacle while carrying a gun. The firearm is opened, unloaded, and carefully handed to a companion or placed on the far side of the fence.

Generally speaking, a gun should be carried with the muzzle pointing up and with the safety button or lever in the "on" position. If it is accidentally dropped or if (for any reason) snow, dirt, or anything else may have entered the muzzle, the gun must be opened and the bore must be inspected to make certain it is not obstructed. Even a partially blocked bore can cause a barrel to rupture upon firing and is very dangerous.

Many writers have compiled sets of rules and given them labels such as the Ten Safety Commandments. They all boil down to common sense and the primary rule that every gun must be treated as if it were loaded.

One last bit of advice for the fledgling duck hunter. Besides a valid state hunting license, you will need a current Migratory Bird Hunting and Conservation Stamp before hunting anywhere in the United States. These can be purchased in any post office. Revenue from sale of the stamps is used in scientific waterfowl management and to acquire wetlands on which waterfowl can live. In other words, you are contributing to better waterfowling in the future when you purchase your stamp.

CHAPTER 7

DUCK AND GOOSE BLINDS

It isn't often that a wind becomes as raw and penetrating as one did on a December morning at Tennessee's Reelfoot Lake, although this was only a couple of good casts from the cotton fields. Nor have I often seen such shooting, because I stood in full view of a constant stream of canvasbacks that roared downwind to reach the stool and the patch of buffalo grass just below me.

The ducks poured in crazily, some close enough for me to feel the rush of wings. It happened that I was standing about fifteen feet

This pit blind is a three-man affair with sliding lids that can be whipped out of the way as geese fly into range and a gunner stands up to shoot. Atop the lids, a thin lattice of dry cornstalks disguises the installation. (*Will Ryan*)

This is a semipermanent but movable blind that serves very well for river shooting. The wooden frame is mounted on skids and the exterior is covered with native willow or grass. The blind can be moved to new locations as water levels or flight patterns change. This particular blind is located on a Mississippi River sandbar near New Madrid, Missouri.

above the water. My blind was merely a small platform—standing room—atop the sawed-off trunk of a cypress tree. To the decoying ducks I guess I resembled part of the tree trunk, and the surrounding limbs were enough to break up any telltale silhouette. I've enjoyed much more comfortable blinds, but not many which were more effective.

A good part of waterfowling success anywhere is the hunter's ability to conceal himself. Ducks and geese have extraordinary vision, and they rate with America's most shy and wary wildlife. They seldom come into shotgun range unless the hunter is hidden or sufficiently disguised.

Adapting to Surroundings

Although building a blind can be a challenge to a sportsman's ingenuity, it is no complicated matter. Ordinarily there are enough natural materials everywhere for the construction. It is up to the hunter to make the best use of these materials, and he should remember that deception is the most vital part of his work. Here is how Frank Vorhees and I solved a typical problem early one season when we spotted a concentration of wood ducks and teal in a pond-and-pothole section in Delaware County, Ohio.

Before the season opened Frank had found an oxbow of a relocated creek where the ducks seemed to loiter for many hours during the day. He placed our blind in the center of the oxbow and on the inside of the curve. The framework was fashioned from saplings, which he cut near the site. Since the slopes surrounding the oxbow were dotted with scarlet sumac, Frank cut pieces of this plant and lashed them to his frame until it resembled another clump of sumac. For several days, until a cold front pushed the bluewings and the wood ducks farther south, we had memorable shooting.

Placement and Camouflage

A blind can be a fairly permanent structure or it can be only temporary, depending on its location. In the marsh or swampy sections along established flyways a permanent blind is more

economical. Where the habits of ducks are not stable, or perhaps just for a one-time shoot, a temporary blind is enough. But for either type, the builder must always keep some important considerations in mind.

The first is the prevailing wind and the flight pattern of the ducks. If they ordinarily approach from one direction, the blind should face that way to give the best field of fire. Waterfowl prefer to face into the wind as they descend and land. Ideally, a blind should be situated so that the prevailing wind crosses it from one side or the other or blows against your back. With a crossing wind, the birds are likely to cross in front of you as they descend for a closer look

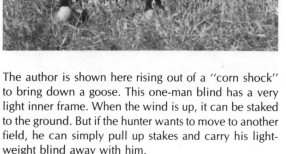

The author is shown here rising out of a "corn shock" to bring down a goose. This one-man blind has a very light inner frame. When the wind is up, it can be staked to the ground. But if the hunter wants to move to another field, he can simply pull up stakes and carry his light-weight blind away with him.

Commercial portable blinds have become popular in heavily gunned public hunting areas where frequent footwork may be needed to find good, uncrowded shooting sites. This one is called the Insta-Blind. It's a tent-style hexagon that weighs only eight pounds and can be set up or taken down and folded in seconds. (*Joann Kirk*)

At the edge of a field, a single wall of thatched grasses, corn, or other vegetation on a wire frame looks like an innocent hedgerow and therefore makes a fine blind. Waiting behind this one for his second goose of the morning is hunting writer Bob Elman. (*Dick Dietz*)

at the decoys or, on occasion, try to drop right in among the decoys. With the wind at your back, birds are likely to approach from out in front of your blind. The toughest shots tend to be at overhead birds that come from behind you—partly because they so often take you by surprise and then flare away before you can get the gun swinging ahead of them.

The exact location of the blind is important too, from the standpoint of access in all sorts of weather. When water levels fall, it's sometimes impossible to hike across miles of mud flats that were easily negotiated by boat before. This is a common problem when hunting ducks in tidal areas. One word to the wise waterfowler. Points of land are nearly always good if they are accessible.

Camouflage is next in importance to placement of the blind. The surrounding scene or landscape should be changed as little as possible. And that means using local materials, a point which cannot be stressed too much. Avoid using materials which clash with the environment—such as green lumber in a permanent marsh blind. It is far better to use scrap or weathered lumber.

When using local grasses and foliage, be certain to gather it some distance away from the blind. And at the same time be sure to duplicate the nearby material so that the immediate area of your blind has no tramped-down or cutover look. These considerations become much more important as the duck season progresses and the ducks become more sophisticated.

Materials

I have found that certain materials, tools, and equipment are so handy in blind building that I would advise the wandering waterfowler to carry them in his car trunk at all times during the fall. These items include a hand ax, a folding shovel, baling wire, Manila twine, burlap sacking, and staples. With these a man can quickly and easily erect a temporary blind almost anywhere.

Chicken wire and three-foot wire garden fencing are extremely valuable too. One duck hunter I know weaves marsh grass into a twelve-foot section of garden wire. All through the season he carries it rolled up in his station wagon. In a few minutes' time he can set up this blind for business just by unrolling the wire and forcing the ends into the soft ground.

Portable Blinds

Some hunters pack along camouflage netting or other camouflage material—often perforated or "ribboned" so that it flutters in the breeze like grass. Various camouflage materials are available at sporting goods stores and by mail order. Available from the same sources are ready-made collapsible blinds—ultralight, compact, and easily portable. Typically, such blinds have frames of aluminum or plastic tubing under camouflage-patterned nylon or some other suitable material. When anchored to the ground securely, a portable blind is an efficient form of concealment that blends well with many natural settings. It can't match a pit blind for concealment, nor is it as roomy, warm, and comfortably appointed as some permanent blinds of various types, but it does have one big advantage. It can be put up in a couple of minutes, then taken down and moved to another site if the wind shifts unfavorably or the shooting is poor where you've set it—and it can go wherever you go in your vehicle. Some portable blinds can even be set up over a small duck boat, and for that matter there are duck boats with built-in collapsible blinds.

All the same, some waterfowlers prefer to fashion their own blinds with whatever suitable materials can be found at hand. Economy may

be the motivation for a few hunters, but I suspect that a good many people simply derive great satisfaction from building things from scratch.

Many good duck-hunting areas are located near waters where commercial fishing is carried on, and this means that fish netting is available. Old and weathered fish netting is a splendid blind material. Spread it across a frame and then weave grass, foliage, or strips of burlap into the

Sometimes camo netting or scrim is all the blind you need. Here, the author prepares to shove off on a float trip down the Missouri River. His party is using inflatable boats for jump-shooting, and they packed thin sheets of camouflage scrim not only to mask the bows of the inflatables but also to prop up as blinds at promising shoreline locations for pass-shooting.

Leafy camouflage mesh (in this case a commercial product called Dukoflage) was originally inspired by military gun emplacements. It's usually reversible, comes in various camo colors and patterns, and utilizes light but extremely tough fabric. It can be draped over a boat, a landbased frame, or a pit. Incidentally, this hunter is shooting a muzzleloading shotgun. Black-powder guns of this sort are used by a small but dedicated number of waterfowlers. (*Joann Kirk*)

In many regions, nothing can beat a traditional waterside blind of upright reeds, rushes, and grasses attached to a wooden frame. The disguise is effective, and inside there's room for a bench, a shelf for ammunition boxes, lunch and hot drinks, and a comfortable corner for the dog. This pintail hunter and his partner (who took the picture) have taken their limits from a Gulf Coast blind of this type. (*Joe Richard*)

net. It is a good idea to take the netting down after every session in the blind, because in bad weather it is easily blown away.

Remember that burlap is also an extremely good camouflage material. It is excellent for covering the blind. Strips of burlap inside a blind also give some insulation and add warmth on bad days.

Along rocky shores and jetties, piled-up rocks can make a natural and effective blind. The hunter can hide behind them or build a four-wall pit which offers protection as well as concealment. Often it is a good idea first to build a framework, perhaps of old wooden timbers or driftwood, and then to pile the rocks roughly around the outside as a stone mason might do. This type of blind is extremely effective around the rocky islands of Lake Erie, and no doubt it would be equally suitable in similar areas elsewhere.

Comfort is important for spending long hours in a blind. But camouflage should be the first consideration. It is a wise waterfowler who keeps the vicinity of his blind policed of empty cigarette packages, sandwich wrappers, shell cases, and other litter that will seem unnatural to a passing duck.

The size of any blind is very important. A space about three feet square will accommodate any but the largest man. A two-man blind, sunken or above water, should be about six feet by three feet and about four feet high. The average man is comfortable on a seat eighteen inches high.

On rocky points, hunters of diving ducks often use a very simple, homemade portable blind—a length of snow fence or wired lathing strips with a curtain of old burlap tacked or stapled over the slats. It's easily rolled up and carried away, and evidently it appears to incoming ducks like just another huge boulder. Look closely at this photo and you'll notice that the hunters have taken a bufflehead and a goldeneye, or whistler. (*Will Ryan*)

This blind, in Maryland, is a traditional type in use all over the United States. The wooden framework is permanent and is large enough so that two hunters can sit comfortably for long periods of time. The outer dressing of grass or cornstalks is refurbished or replaced each year.

Sunken Blinds

Wherever the location will permit, pit or sunken blinds are at least as effective as any built above ground. Depending upon the situation and the need for permanence, they can be built for standing or sitting. In some goose-hunting locales, waterfowlers literally lie in wait for approaching birds—they lie more or less flat on their backs in shallow trenches, then sit up fast to shoot. Pits can be simple earth excavations or they can be made from sunken barrels. Where drainage is no problem, they can be lined inside with concrete blocks. The covers or lids can be anything from cornstalks to mats of woven grass to synthetic turf. The hunter shoots from a sitting position or throws off the lid and jumps up to shoot.

For permanent installation in the ground, there are also factory-made steel drums, widely known as "Smitty blinds" in reference to one famous brand. These drums generally have a ground-level lid that can be swung aside for shooting. Grass, cornstalks, etc., can be secured atop the lid to disguise it. Inside the drum there is a seat, and usually a rail that can serve as a

These hunters are taking advantage of natural cover by using cypress trees on Tennessee's Reelfoot Lake as blinds. Platforms are built in the trees or atop the stumps. A motionless hunter blends into the tree trunk and resembles just another dead limb. Ducks in the area are accustomed to seeing these cypress "ghosts" and will not take alarm unless the hunter moves.

This Florida hunter, watching for mallards to descend on a tangled oak forest, has camouflaged himself with Spanish moss, a natural material very abundant in the area.

Here's another of the innovative, store-bought portable blinds. Called the Goose Trap, it weighs only 12½ pounds, stands only 15 inches high when its legs are staked into the ground, and is easily folded and transported. This one-man blind is reminiscent of a layout boat, since the hunter lies on his back to watch the sky for incoming ducks or geese. The camouflage mesh cover does not obstruct his view. The head end of the contrivance works like a spring-loaded trapdoor, flipping open 180 degrees when the gunner pushes it and sits up to shoot.

This hunter uses an old wooden beverage crate as a handy seat in his blind. The compartments hold duck and goose calls, shells, snacks, candy, gloves, etc. A vacuum jug of hot beverage will be welcome when a raw wind begins to blow.

foot rest or a handy shelf for a shell box. From a pit blind of this type, a gunner can see—and shoot—in all directions.

Sunken blinds are most effective where the terrain is flat, such as in grainfields from which the grain has been harvested.

A sunken barrel can be located in open water as well as on dry land. But there is a trick to doing it. The barrel is filled with water to sink it and is fastened to stakes driven into the bottom beside it. Then the barrel is pumped dry.

Only the ingenuity of an outdoorsman limits the potential of effective blind building. Some gunners I've known have even planted and grown their own blinds. One waterfowler I knew in Mississippi erected a permanent blind and then transplanted honeysuckle, an evergreen plant, all around it. The honeysuckle grew and enveloped the blind. The hunter needed only to trim out a shooting space at the beginning of each season.

In Florida I knew another sportsman who sawed off a large, dead cypress five feet above the water line. It was partially decayed and hollowed out, so the man only whittled away until he had enough space to sit inside, almost completely hidden. Many pintails and mallards were bagged from that stump.

Floating Blinds and Boat Blinds

And then there are floating blinds. Many of those mentioned so far can be mounted on steel oil drums or pontoons and anchored wherever ducks are flying. An alternative to the floating blind is the stake blind, which the hunter can build by cutting saplings and arranging them in a circle in the water. The hunter then stands hidden in the center of the circle. Of course, hip boots or waders are necessary for this type of structure. A better type for permanent use is built *over* the water, on pilings, with a nice dry floor.

Sometimes it may be necessary to use a boat as a blind. However, there are drawbacks. One is the element of danger when two gunners shoot from a small boat.

If you use a boat for tidewater shooting, be sure you have reliable information on tides. It has been the unhappy experience of many gunners to find the perfect spot among the reeds with only a foot or two of water, and then to have the tide run out. That could mean spending a cold and miserable six to eight hours or more waiting for the tide to come in again before it is possible to move the boat to open water.

The use of a boat for a blind is far more acceptable on lakes where water levels do not fluctuate. On many rivers a boat can be successfully concealed beneath overhanging trees or alders if it does not have its own built-in blind. Elsewhere the boat can be camouflaged with natural material gathered nearby on the bank. An inverted boat can also be used; Glenn Lau and I have done this while "laying out" for ducks and geese on small reefs and rock piles in Lake Erie.

A blind should be built as long as possible before you plan to use it. This is particularly true of a permanent blind. This gives waterfowl a chance to get used to it and accept it as part of the scene.

CHAPTER 8

WATERFOWL DECOYS

A thousand years ago in the Southwest, an Indian sat in a cave and fashioned counterfeit canvasback ducks. He formed the head and body of reeds, bound them tightly with bulrushes, and colored them with pigments. Finally he stuck feathers into the body to make it as lifelike as possible.

The finished products are now the world's oldest known waterfowl decoys, discovered in Lovelock Cave, Nevada, in 1911. Today they are in the collection of New York's Museum of the American Indian.

Similar reed counterfeits attracted wild ducks into the range of primitive Indian weapons—throw nets or bows and arrows—and decoys have been in use ever since. Only the design and the materials have changed: from reeds, mud, and skins, to wood, cork, cloth, rubber, and modern plastics. But no matter what the material, decoys are almost as important to duck hunters today as their guns.

History

The story of decoys and decoy making has all the romance and color of the history of America. There is a close parallel, in fact, because waterfowling is a traditional sport. Settlers in the seventeenth century were faced with an endless search for food. The decoys they copied from the Indians made the search a bit easier. But the reed and duckskin decoys blew away during bad weather (when waterfowling is often best), and some anonymous settlers began whittling wooden decoys.

The first whittled models were merely rough wooden affairs in the general shape of swimming ducks. They were called blocks or stools, the latter from "stool pigeon," a device long used to attract and trap pigeons in the Old World. (The word "stool" is now sometimes used to mean an entire rig or pattern of decoys.) The word "decoy" didn't come into use until

This is one of the prehistoric decoys discovered in Nevada's Lovelock Cave in 1911. It was used more than a millenium ago by hunters known to archaeologists as the Tule Eaters—believed to be ancestors of the Northern Paiutes. Some of the feather covering remains intact on this mummy-like decoy, which was fashioned mostly of reeds and bulrushes. It measures 11¼ inches long. (*The Museum of the American Indian, Heye Foundation*)

For many years, hunters throughout the country have used pieces of old automobile tires to fashion field decoys for geese. They're painted white for snows, but ordinary unpainted black works for Canadas. An appropriately painted flat wooden head-and-neck unit is inserted through a slit in the rubber, and the lower end of the wooden unit often forms a stake that anchors it. Such decoys are heavy enough to remain stable without a stake in any weather milder than a gale. With the heads removed, the rubber-tire bodies can be stacked compactly, but they are cumbersome to carry. (*Gene Hornbeck, Nebraska Game Commission*)

after 1800; it comes from the contraction of Dutch words which mean duck cage or trap.

In the early days of settlement on the Eastern Seaboard, waterfowl were less sophisticated than they are today. Young birds especially would drop into decoys which only remotely resembled live ducks. As hunting increased and the ducks got smarter, better decoys were needed. One result was that decoy making became a specialized craft and some decoy makers became artists in the truest sense of the word.

Not only were the body shapes true and graceful, but each decoy was carefully painted. Today some of their original decoys are as valuable as fine paintings. They bring astronomical bids at auctions which attract collectors from all parts of the country.

By 1850 or thereabouts, decoy making was a recognized and highly important profession. A single hunter might use as many as five hundred decoys, and there are records of much larger "spreads" in the Susquehanna River flats and

These are "windsock" stick-ups made by North Wind Decoys. Even in a light breeze, the bodies fill out and move slightly, wobbling and bobbing like feeding geese. Note that some of them also have fluttering wings. They may not look totally realistic to the human eye, but they are extremely effective in fooling waterfowl. They are also about the lightest and most easily transported of all decoys. (*Joann Kirk*)

in Chesapeake Bay. Definite regional types also began to appear.

The Stratford and Housatonic River area of Connecticut became know for exquisite decoys. Barnegat Bay decoys were hollow (and therefore lighter), so that a hunter could carry more of them. Miniature models appeared in portions of New England; the small size was less conspicuous and less likely to betray hunters who violated laws against Sunday shooting.

Decoy making wasn't confined to ducks alone. Some craftsmen specialized in geese, both building full-bodied models and the flat silhouette decoys which are still used today. In addition there were swan, curlew, rail, dowitcher, plover, coot, snipe, and heron decoys. A number of very old, quaint loon decoys are in existence. So are gull stools, but these are considered "confidence decoys" rather than an attempt to entice gulls into gunning range. The theory was (and is) that gulls give circling ducks

enough confidence to come closer. Thus the ducks are "gulled," so to speak.

The end of the nineteenth century marked the greatest era of waterfowl gunning ever known on earth. Besides the sportsmen, market hunters were operating everywhere, and the need for decoys was immense. Even though live ducks were being used as stools, the demand for artificials was so great that factories rather than individual artists began to produce many of them.

During the Civil War the first rubber decoys appeared. Soon after, a quacking decoy was patented. The quacking was caused by a bellows worked by wave action. Still later came tipup decoys, operated with strings or pulleys, to simulate ducks feeding on the surface.

A few hunters may still use and swear by decoys that can be moved by pulling on a long string from inside the blind, but most of us feel that a well-placed spread of well-made decoys

Carry-Lite decoys, like the North Wind windsocks, come in both standard and "magnum" sizes, but they exemplify a different concept in current decoy manufacture. They're formed of tough, molded polyethylene, and although they appear solid they're collapsible for easy transport and storage. Made in Italy, these full-bodied decoys are imported by such companies as L.L. Bean. They come in floater form as well as field decoys, and in addition to the snow geese and Canadas there are Carry-Lite mallards, blacks, scaup, pintails, teal, and wood ducks. (*Courtesy of L.L. Bean, Freeport, Maine*)

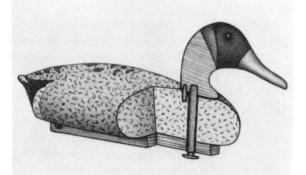

This cutaway drawing shows the construction of the cork-bodied decoys marketed by L.L. Bean. The head and a small tail insert are handshaped wood, and the keel is rubber-coated wood. A small, hidden "collar" device permits rotation of the head to three different realistic positions, and a hardwood dowel extends through the keel and body into the neck to add strength. Such decoys are extremely durable and stable. (*Drawing Courtesy of L.L. Bean, Freeport, Maine*)

needs no such embellishments. Other kinds of gadgetry come and go. Not long ago, a battery-powered, remote-controlled swimming decoy appeared on the market. It was even equipped with a clasping device so that it could (supposedly) retrieve downed birds for the gunner. There may be some question as to whether such devices are legal, but there's no question about their absurdity.

Oversized decoys, called magnums, cannot be classified as mere gadgets. They're cumbersome but effective, probably because they can be seen and recognized by waterfowl at long distances. Every few years someone builds (and occasionally even markets) a truly gigantic hollow decoy that dwarfs the magnums and is, in fact, so capacious that a gunner can hide inside it. More often than not, this is done as a joke. No further comment is needed.

Wood, Cork, Plastic, Fabric

Among the old-time carvers of realistic decoys, cedar was the most popular wood. Long ago, someone decided to try cork instead of cedar for floating decoys (as opposed to those used on land), and a cork floater is still unbeatable if properly made, painted, and weighted. Some hunters even prefer cork for stickup decoys on land. Quite a few artists and home craftsmen still make their own cork decoys, and a few even carve them of wood—although most of today's carvers use wood only for beautifully sculptured decorative decoys and not for true working decoys that will be knocked about, weathered, and shot over. Excellent factory-made cork decoys are still available, too. They cost much more than the molded synthetic "dekes," but there are hunters who can afford them and want nothing less. The famous firm of L.L. Bean, for instance, markets cork-bodied ducks and geese as well as synthetic ones.

Well-made cork-bodied decoys have excellent balance and just the right buoyancy to ride the water realistically. (*Joann Kirk*)

These are taxidermy decoys—"stuffed" geese mounted in various lifelike postures on small wooden platforms. They are surprisingly durable and they represent the ultimate in realism, but they are necessarily costly (or unnecessarily, if you feel as most gunners do that machine-made counterfeits attract just as many birds). (*Will Ryan*)

Serious sportsmen sometimes go to extremes for the sake of good goose shooting. An example was Glenn L. Martin, a pioneer of American aviation who hunted geese in the grand style and with the ultimate in decoys. After the use of live decoys was banned many years ago, he used wild honkers mounted by a taxidermist in natural feeding, resting, and sentinel postures. That tradition is carried on today by a few waterfowlers who can afford it. I know of a successful real estate investor in Maryland who invites friends to shoot with him from large and elaborate sunken blinds on his farm. Before sunup on the morning of a shoot, flatbed trailers trundle perhaps a hundred "stuffed" Canada geese out to the shooting site. The host is so gracious that his shoots would be marvelous regardless of the decoys, but there's no doubt these taxidermy decoys are very effective, and shooting over them is a memorable experience. Curiously, however, a lot of serious goose hunters bag their limits just as consistently with well-placed but simple silhouette decoys cut from plywood.

When the first edition of this book was published in 1965, rubber decoys were frequently seen and papier-mâché decoys were quite popular. Those materials have been eclipsed by today's much more durable plastics—chiefly polyethylene, which is light, nearly indestructible, easily molded with realistic feather patterns and textures, and takes non-reflective, realistic paints. When properly keeled and weighted, this kind of decoy floats and bobs in a lifelike way, and rights itself if knocked over.

Typical and very popular are the Carry-Lite synthetic ducks and geese, which are stable on water, include a variety of species—even a confidence gull—and are so light that a waterfowler can, without straining himself, carry far more than he could tote if he were using old-style blocks.

Extremely realistic "field shells" are the landbound counterparts of the floaters. You can make a fine land decoy by cutting an old automobile tire in half, painting it appropriately, and adding a neck and head of painted wood or any other suitable material. But a lot of us who have shot geese for decades over tire decoys remember their weight as vividly as their effectiveness. We are therefore thankful for the

Simple, cheap, and traditional surf-scoter silhouettes are effective for luring scoters and other sea ducks. For example, they attracted the pair of eiders lying atop the lobster traps in this picture. (*Tom Shoener, Maine Fish & Game Department*)

light plastic field shells. The heads come in feeding and upright versions and can be rotated to vary their positions for added realism. The head/neck units are instantly detachable, and the Carry-Lite shells—that is, the bodies—can then be nestled or stacked for fast, easy carrying and storage. The same decoys are available in full-bodied versions, but I prefer the flat-bottomed shells for their stacking convenience; they seem to be equally attractive to geese.

Another outstanding development of recent years has been the introduction of "windsock" field decoys. I believe this ingenious construction was pioneered by North Wind Decoys,

For generations, homemade goose decoys have been fashioned from chicken wire, painted cloth, and a wooden stake to form the neck; the decoys anchor to the ground, and hold a roughly carved and painted wooden head. Such decoys work very well, though to the human eye they appear primitive. (*Gene Hornbeck, Nebraska Game Commission*)

tance, it looks like a bird in the act of landing. These windsocks are as lightweight as a decoy can get, and you can easily tuck a whole batch of them under one arm on the way to or from the field.

On a totally still day, windsock decoys sag, and to the human eye they look about as lifelike as a limp sock hanging on a clothesline. Yet they still seem to attract ducks and geese (though not nearly as effectively as on a breezy day). There are two ways to solve the problem of becalmed windsocks. One is to use a mixed spread, sprinkling them among polyethylene or other stiff-bodied decoys. The other is to buy inexpensive accessory supports that fit inside the socks to hold their shape on still days. For all I know, the original windsock idea may have been inspired by the homemade goose decoys that were fashioned years ago by stretching cloth over a slat or chicken-wire frame and then painting it. Those decoys worked too.

Mass Produced vs. Homemade

The mass-produced decoys in use today certainly don't have the elegance, beauty, and individualistic style of the old wooden decoys, but they are far more convenient and easy to use, reasonably priced, and very effective. The old handsome cedar and cork counterfeits are now far more valuable as collector's items than as working decoys. If you stumble across one in an attic, barn, or abandoned duck club, you should probably try to have its maker identified by a reputable dealer or collector, and then have it appraised for insurance.

Many sportsmen wonder whether it is worth the time and trouble to make their own decoys for duck or goose shooting. The answer in most cases is probably that it is. Mass-produced decoys can be sturdy, durable, and even very effective, but it is impossible to match the authenticity and style which a waterfowler can produce in his own home workshop. But more than this is the satisfaction of making a counterfeit of your own which will one day attract a flock a ducks within easy shooting range. There are a number of good books that outline step-by-step how to make decoys for all species of ducks.

though it's possible that more or less similar stickups may be manufactured by other companies if they can be produced without danger of patent infringement. The body of a North Wind decoy is merely a shell of synthetic cloth—just like the windsocks used at airports to indicate wind direction. It's attached at the top of a leg, or stake, that holds it upright above the ground. Also at the top of the stake, a molded, adjustable head is attached. The body and head swivel about the stake, facing into the breeze and gently fluttering like real birds. There's also a "hovering" version with inflatable wings jutting from the body. From a dis-

A duck hunter on Sandusky Bay, Ohio, uses piles of mud to supplement regular black and mallard decoys.

Placement, Number, and Variety

The proper placement of decoys and the arrangement of good stool is a subject for controversy wherever two or more duck hunters gather. Ducks are about as unpredictable as trout in heavily fished waters. To say that one type of placement will work is about like saying a certain fly will always catch trout. Trout fisherman know there is no such fly.

Let's see what it is that makes waterfowl come to artificial decoys. To begin with, they are gregarious critters and would rather be with other ducks of their own kind than alone. No doubt the sight of other ducks on the water gives assurance to approaching ducks that there is no danger below. It suggests the presence of food, too.

There is good evidence that the more authentic the decoy, the more readily ducks will come in to it. However, ducks and geese are known to decoy to everything from rusty tin cans and mounds of mud to pieces of rubber tire and old cardboard boxes. In Canada, I have seen Cree Indians use sticks and mud, the skins of dead birds, dead birds propped up, and just the wings of birds fastened to sticks.

Many times a waterfowler will find himself far from a source of decoys, and it is well to

A goose hunter makes silhouette decoys in a basement workshop. These painted plywood "shadow decoys" are easy and inexpensive to make—and effective as well.

Stickup silhouettes can be used in very shallow water as well as on land. The stakes are driven into the bottom just far enough so that the decoys seem to be standing in or floating on the water. (*Rick Methot*)

These very old handcarved canvasback decoys have retained their paint well and probably would float beautifully, but they're far too valuable as collector's items to be used as "working" decoys.

bluebills—more decoys invariably mean better shooting.

Although ducks may be more susceptible to a spread of decoys simulating their own species, most ducks will decoy to unidentified species. Otherwise why would any duck ever come in close to blobs of mud or to decoys made out of cardboard boxes? Some birds not in the waterfowl family or entirely different kinds of waterfowl actually seem to give certain ducks confidence. For example, it is an old-time trick when hunting puddle ducks to include Canada geese or coot or a few gull decoys around the fringe of the decoys. All kinds of ducks often pour into areas where there are concentrations of wild geese. They will do the same thing if there are goose decoys among the duck decoys.

No doubt a gunner's best bet is to observe wild ducks whenever he has the opportunity and see how they deport and place themselves when resting on the water. For example, feeding

Molded polyethylene decoys are light enough so that you can carry a full rig of "puddlers" in a sturdy mesh decoy bag. (L.L. Bean, Freeport, Maine)

remember that some of these simple things will work. As in any phase of duck hunting, ingenuity in preparing and setting out decoys can mean the difference between success and failure.

Speaking of waterfowling in general, ducks and geese will decoy best to large numbers of their own kind. In other words, the more decoys on the water, the better the chances of pulling in birds. An exception to this is in hunting the shallow-water ducks on small streams or along potholes. Also, approaching teal or wood ducks might find it more natural if only a few ducks were previously on the pond. In hunting the diving ducks—canvasbacks, redheads, and

An Indian decoy of mud and sticks—suitable in a pinch when conventional dekes aren't handy.

puddle ducks will ordinarily not bunch together. They will be scattered out evenly over an area, no two ducks very close together. This, then, should be the way puddle-duck decoys are arranged before a shoot.

Among the common tricks of setting out decoys for the diving ducks is to arrange them in a pattern so that an open space exists among the decoys and this open space is within easy shooting range of the blind. The actual formation might be an oval, it might be heartshaped or fishhook-shaped. In any case, there must be ample space for new arrivals to land in the center of the blocks.

Tossing out the decoys in relation to the blind might be more important than any other factor in proper placement. Remember that nearly all ducks when making a final approach toward

decoys will come upwind. The blind therefore should be located so that a shooter can take advantage of this approach and have the best possible open shot at the approaching birds. A very common mistake is to place the decoys too far from the blind. This kind of stool is of little value because decoying ducks will settle far out of range and will either furnish the shooter with no action at all or will cause him to take longer than sensible shots, which will only cripple game.

Some gunners make a point of placing one decoy somewhat apart from the rest and at a fairly precise distance of forty yards from the blind. It serves as a range marker, because the shooter knows that any duck or goose flying over or near it is within range. Since range estimation is often difficult, this is a good idea.

There are other little details about the placement of decoys that most experienced waterfowlers keep in mind. If it is midday, for example, and you're shooting puddle ducks, always place a few individual decoys on the shore, or on dry land, because it is the habit of puddle ducks to rest in this manner. It is doubly characteristic on warm days.

Be sure that decoys are always well anchored and that at least at the beginning of the season strong new cord is used to tie between decoy and anchor. Many a valuable decoy has been lost in a strong wind or storm because last year's decayed line was used. Also, be certain the lines are not white or bright in color, because in clear water these are telltale signs to approaching ducks that all is not well below.

Entire volumes have been written on the proper placement of waterfowl decoys. But it really boils down to the individual shooter's ingenuity and to his instinct for what will more quickly and more effectively attract waterfowl within shooting range. Some days the ducks will make a man feel he is truly an expert and that he has at last mastered decoy placement. On other days they will make him wish he had stayed home.

CHAPTER 9

FREELANCING FOR WATERFOWL

Although some of the best wildfowling areas—marshes, deltas, and wet lowlands on major flyways—are in private ownership, there is still plenty of opportunity for any enterprising scattergunner. It's not always a cut-and-dried case of slipping into a prepared blind at daybreak and waiting for rafts of mallards to struggle upwind into a grand spread of decoys. Nor is it sustained pass-shooting where ducks funnel past a strategic spot from feeding to resting grounds. It's neither easy nor predictable. But it *is* productive and can be very exciting.

Farm Ponds

Take the farm ponds. There are nearly three quarters of a million of them across America's landscape. Ducks drop in on them and evidently like what they find, for they stay until they're disturbed. Getting a limit often is a matter of properly hunting a couple of ponds. Here's how:

First obtain the landowner's permission. That's usually not difficult if you use the same courtesy and approach you use in other matters. After that, it's a test of how good an infantryman you would make.

Inadvertently, of course, farm ponds were as well designed for duck hunters as they were for storing water. Typical construction places a low dam across a small, shallow drainage. By approaching from downstream and keeping below the crest of the dam, perhaps by crawling and creeping, a hunter can approach to within shotgun range of the birds without ever being seen.

When he stands up or rises to his knees to shoot, the birds leap into the air as if flung from a catapult. In reference to this sudden flush of alarmed birds, the method has come to be called jump-shooting. If the hunter is a good shot, he'll take a couple on the flush. If not, it was good practice for the next try.

Jump-Shooting and Decoying

A two-man team can work the farm-pond ducks just as effectively—maybe more so. While one man crawls up from the dam side, another makes a wide circle out of sight and begins a crawling stalk from the upstream side. The ducks are sandwiched and one gunner is almost certain to have action.

Crawling is an art in itself and for some of these farm ponds with very low dams, you'd better learn how. In a prone position, lay your gun across the crook in your elbow. Carry it right there. Keeping your head and buttocks down, move forward by advancing the left elbow and left knee, then your right elbow and right knee at the same time. It's slow and tedious but it's as good for sneaking up on ducks as it was for its original purpose of infiltrating enemy positions.

Traditionally, most American hunters have used carrying slings only on rifles, but Europeans like them on shotguns as well. More and more Americans now use detachable slings on shotguns for waterfowling, and such a sling is an excellent accessory for jump-shooting. In some situations, the gun can be carried by the

This hunter has equipped his shotgun with a carrying sling, which can be very useful in waterfowling, and all the more so when you're freelancing for ducks. You'll often be moving about and will want both hands free. The parka he's wearing (a Cabela Gore-Tex Waterfowler's Parka) is also a good choice. Unlike many of the old-style duck-hunting coats, it has a built-in game bag for carrying your ducks, and it's waterproof, light, and warm.

sling while the hunter stalks his way into flushing position. (Just take care never to drag the gun in a manner that will allow any mud, snow, or ground debris to get into its muzzle or action.) It's after the shooting that the sling is most useful, for a jump-shooter may have to carry a limit of ducks or geese a long distance back to his car. For that matter, a hunter using decoys may also be very thankful for a sling since it frees both hands for carrying home a sack of decoys as well as bagged birds.

But that's still not the whole farm-pond story.

Find a pond that's located near larger waters where ducks concentrate in great numbers and you've found a fine spot to pitch out a few blocks. Put up a hasty blind and sit for a few hours early and late in the day—perhaps all day if the weather raises too rough a chop for the ducks to rest out on open water. The birds will gradually filter in to find more quiet places. That's when you can collect a few in duck-club style. Group your decoys loosely in a sheltered place.

If you're using decoys, why not try something a little more effective than the usual motionless spread? Place a heavy anchor or weight with an "eye" in the center of the blocks. Run a Manila or other hemp or nylon line from your blind, through the eye of the anchor, and tie it to the bill of a decoy floating just over the anchor. When ducks come in range, pull gently on the line, causing the block to tip up like a duck feeding. Some hunters declare this string-activated rig to be a real magnet, particularly when the water is calm.

There is a lot more to good duck hunting than the actual shooting. It's fascinating, and legal, to start before the season opens. Just leave your shooting iron at home and tote a pair of binoculars instead. Methodically, whenever there's a little spare time, reconnoiter every patch of water in your neighborhood where shooting is permitted. Some flights usually arrive in every region before opening day, so make it a point to know just where they are and what they're doing. Check all the inconsequential ponds, sloughs, potholes, creeks, rivers—the works. Visit some farmers and inquire about hunting on their ponds. Get a county map (most county engineers or surveyors have them available) if necessary to locate waters you've never known about. Look especially for newly flooded woods and croplands; these are terrific.

Now it's eve of opening day. You know where the most ducks are loitering. You know which place is the easiest to approach. So make your choice and be sitting there quietly when day begins to break—or at the opening hour, whenever that is in your state. You should have action soon.

It's important to be well hidden when you wait for that opening hour. But it's not difficult even without a blind. Just wear camo-pattern hunting clothes and hide yourself in brush or

There are many ways to float for ducks (and for geese as well on some waterways). At top, the author and his wife and friends prepare to board inflatables for a gunning trip down the Missouri River in Montana. At left below, a hunter prepares to load the Toobie Camouflage Hunting & Fishing Boat, marketed by Land, Air, & Water Sports Equipment in Imperial Beach, California. This is a compact, light, but sturdy inflatable that can be maneuvered in water as shallow as 18 inches with either a gasoline outboard or electric trolling motor. It features a canopy-type detachable blind with a quick-release lever. The blind can be instantly collapsed to give the hunter a clear line of fire. At right below is that most traditional of float-hunting craft—a canoe whose bow has been festooned with burlap and foliage for camouflage.

This hunter, Mike Nauer, uses a floater bubble, sometimes called a "belly-boat," plus insulated waders, a camouflage suit, and a swimmer's flippers on his feet to float downstream for ducks.

Tom Henderson's Tintex "pond" (described in this chapter) on a central Ohio stream, with the decoys he arranged on the fake pond. Henderson is crouched on the ice at left.

Lon Parker spreading his polyethylene pond on a pasture.

other natural cover. Some gunners even emulate bow hunters by daubing their faces with camouflage makeup. Sit still, absolutely still, until action develops. Use a hand warmer if necessary to make you more comfortable and less restless. If the cover and vegetation around the pond are suitable, take a small folding canvas chair to make being immobile easier. Good insulated clothing, by the way, is a blessing when you want to sit still in cold weather.

Rivers and Creeks

For some reason, many wildfowlers neglect the rivers. Perhaps it's because the ducks are hidden too well behind the bends of a mean-

dering waterway and the impression is that no ducks are there at all. But that's rarely true, for some ducks—even geese—seem to prefer water that moves.

Certainly hunting the rivers isn't always an easy matter. If the water is low it means carrying equipment over deadfalls, around rapids, and through shallow bars, and lugging a boat or canoe to and from the water. But these are small hardships for the sport a clever gunner will enjoy during a float trip.

The ideal way to hunt a river is by drifting. You put a boat in at one point and float downstream, perhaps between bridges. You can use two cars or arrange to be picked up by someone else at closing time. A rowboat is by far the most comfortable, but a canoe is most maneuverable

This photo should erase any doubt that mallards will try to drop in among the decoys on a "pond" made of plastic sheeting.

and easiest to handle around obstacles. But a canoe is also less stable when shooting suddenly develops around a bend. Take your choice and proceed with care.

Few ducks will allow an uncamouflaged craft to drift close enough for a shot. So there's work to be done before shoving off. There are many ways to disguise the outline of boat and hunters (which should be the main consideration) simply by using materials around a riverbank, plus plenty of heavy cord. Cut a supply of willows or native grasses. Weave or tie this material together as densely as possible with the cord and

then encircle the boat or canoe with it, tying it to the gunwale at intervals. When the finished product looks like a pile of brush or driftwood at a hundred feet, you're ready to start collecting the legal limit.

Drift freely as much as possible. Never use oars, and use paddles as sparingly as possible when ducks are in sight. When approaching a bend or curve in the river, stay as close as you can to the inside bank. It will give a better shot at birds suddenly flushing when you surprise them.

Here's a stratagem that often pays off when

Wearing waders, this freelancing hunter has been working his way around an Ohio farm pond. He's looking skyward toward far-flying birds that may not come in, but he already has a brace of ducks.

Mallards are among the ducks most often taken by freelancing in farm country. This hunter was well rewarded for slogging through big, muddy, pond-dotted fields. (*Rick Methot*)

Shortly after daybreak, a hunter picks up his second duck. Waterfowl move out to feed very early in the morning, so the best hunting often occurs soon after legal shooting hours begin. You must consult your state's annual tables of legal hours or sunrise/sunset times on which such hours are based (typically from half an hour before official sunrise to official sunset). For example, if a New Jersey hunter had planned to be on his favorite marsh on November 25, 1987, his state's sunrise/sunset tables would have confirmed that he was allowed to bag ducks that day from 6:26 A.M. to 4:36 P.M.

floating. Keep an eye peeled for waterfowl far ahead. As soon as you spot them, swing to the nearest shore, where one hunter can disembark. As soon as that hunter has had time to make a wide swing to get far below the ducks you spotted, push out into the stream and begin the drift again. It's the old sandwich play, which more often than not, if he's well hidden, drives the ducks right past the hunter who made the circle on foot.

The gunner drifting on rivers often encounters a brilliant, furtive bird—the wood duck—that many feel is far superior to any of his cousins once he's plucked and ready for the table. Mallards also love to loaf on rivers and creeks. Same for the bluewing teal, which also keeps to sluggish rivers and to small secluded ponds. Add the tasty ruddy to the list too.

Grainfield Geese

Even geese are available to the average gunner if he'll spend a little time and concentration on locating them. Canadas especially are creatures of habit. Assume a flight of honkers has dropped into a lake near where you live. They'll probably stay until the place freezes, or until they strip the fields of grain, or until the pressure of hunters becomes too annoying. Just remember it doesn't take a large flock of honkers too long to clean up the available feed.

Morning and evening the geese will fly to the same grainfields to feed until something interrupts the flight. Most often that will be a clever hunter who has watched them just long enough to see which way they go. The next time they go, he's waiting conveniently along the flyway or at the feeding site with a spread of decoys. Any gunner can do the same after a little reconnaissance.

The matter of decoys for these grainfield geese is a small problem, really. Silhouettes cut from plywood, the more the better, do the job as well as full-bodied decoys, which are more expensive. Cutting them out of scrap material is a routine job for a home-workshop fan.

Concealment is important in waiting out geese. But it's no problem. Camouflage clothing will help greatly. So will covering up carefully with cornstalks if your vigil happens to take place in a field of harvested corn. You're making

Most hunters associate jump-shooting exclusively with ducks, but the same scouting and stalking methods will also bag geese. Using cattails and other high reeds as cover, this Montana hunter easily sneaked within range before several honkers became alarmed and flew. He bagged one, and should be able to repeat the performance if he has the stamina to keep slogging through the shallows.

like an infantryman, so why not carry a folding shovel and dig in? It will make your concealment all the harder to detect by decoying geese.

At sunrise one raw morning a few years ago, my friend Lon Parker enjoyed a strange brand of duck shooting he never knew before. He bagged a limit of mallards on a pond he had built himself only half an hour before. Then he rolled up the pond and went home for breakfast. I thought it was a practical joke when he told me about it later. But several days afterward he showed me exactly how it worked.

Probably the pioneer in building these counterfeit ponds was Harold Hann, a veteran Kansas City sportsman, who built his ponds with commercial polyethylene sheeting. He selected a cornfield where ducks were accustomed to feed, spread the sheeting, which is available at any building supply store, and pegged it down around the edges to keep it from blowing away. Then he placed a good spread of decoys on the "water" and sat down to wait, either in a shallow pit blind or just underneath the "water."

From the air the polyethylene glitters like the water in a wintry marsh on a windy day. I've flown overhead to see for myself. A fresh wind is helpful, too, because it ripples the sheeting realistically enough to tempt ducks at least into good gunning range. Occasionally they drop down all the way and seem surprised only when they discover the water isn't wet.

Rolled up or folded, enough polyethylene sheeting for a pond is light enough to be carried under the arm, on a sled, or lashed to a packboard. A station wagon can haul a forty- or fifty-foot simulated lake. A pickup truck will do the same job.

Almost every year in many northern states, the duck hunting ends before the legal closing of the season. It can happen when all open water, especially on the smaller ponds and marshes, finally freezes solid. After that, most ducks in any locality move farther south or they congregate far out on the open water of larger lakes, and then commute daily to inland feeding grounds, usually in grainfields. An Ohio sportsman, Tom Henderson, figured out a way to prolong his own shooting until the season is closed officially. His discovery may be suitable to duck-hunting situations elsewhere.

Henderson creates a counterfeit opening on river ice or on a farm pond. It's as elementary as dissolving several boxes of blue Tintex dye in buckets of warm water. These he pours on the ice and the result is a completely genuine-looking blue patch of "open" water on a pond. After he places decoys all around, he has a spread which very few ducks can pass up when the rest of the landscape is frozen tight.

Henderson has found that it isn't even necessary to build a blind out on the ice. Instead he simply covers himself and huddles nearby on the sled (painted white) he uses to carry decoys and a thermos of hot coffee. Snow-goose hunters often wear white coveralls, even when there's no snow on the ground. I suppose we'll never know whether the geese, seeing these blobs of white from above, perceive them as patches of snow or little bunches of their fellow geese feeding in the fields. In any event, white coveralls are equally effective camouflage when hunting ducks from a shooting site on ice or snow. Even a white bedsheet can serve as camouflage—and I saw a hunter draped in one at Henderson's place.

The true test for Henderson's Tintex pond came on the last day of the season. At that late date every duck in the Midwest should have been an expert in detecting counterfeits. Still, Henderson quickly bagged his limit, and then sat in amazement as waterfowl continued to drop in all morning long.

CHAPTER 10

WATERFOWL DOGS

Everywhere during the past few decades there has been increasing emphasis on waterfowl management. As a result, federal, state, and even private agencies have collected data on how many birds are bagged and how many birds are lost. It appears that over the years our national average for waterfowl loss by crippling is as high as 25 percent. That is a disgraceful waste.

This annual loss cuts drastically into our breeding stock of waterfowl as well as into the number of birds we can safely shoot each fall. It's a poor business and poor sportsmanship to allow a fourth of our total waterfowl kill to go down a rat hole because of carelessness.

There are a number of reasons for this terrible waste in waterfowl. One reason is trigger-happy shooting, a matter which has been discussed elsewhere. Another reason is the inability to judge distance or range of ducks. Poor marksmanship is a third factor. But just as important is the failure to retrieve crippled birds.

Some birds, it is sad to report, are not retrieved because the shooters are too lazy to wade through the deep muck of an average marsh. Others retrieve only those birds which are most desirable to eat, and leave the rest on the water. There is absolutely no excuse for this kind of waste and culprits should be dealt with severely when caught. But by far the greatest number of birds are not retrieved for lack of a good dog.

The Dog's Role in Conservation

It is almost impossible to overemphasize the value of a good dog in any kind of waterfowling.

A dog is a pleasure to watch, a companion, and a very valuable ally. Some of the greatest moments I can remember were the "impossible" retrieves made by duck dogs I've known. A dog with a working life of, say, ten or twelve seasons may save hundreds of injured ducks and geese that would otherwise be wasted. Think how many birds can be saved by a hundred thousand dogs and you'll appreciate the role of retrievers in conservation.

Many breeds have been used to retrieve waterfowl, but only a few of them are totally qualified to do this job. Since a large percentage of retrieving must be done from water, which is usually icy or extremely cold, dogs must be especially adapted by their build and constitution to this work. An average house dog might not even be able to endure a long day in a boat or blind under typical duck-hunting conditions. But a good retriever can plunge into icy water time and again and really seem to enjoy the work.

The breeds of dogs most frequently used to retrieve wildfowl today are the Labrador retriever, golden retriever, Chesapeake, springer spaniel, and (less commonly) the American water spaniel, Irish water spaniel, flat-coated retriever, and curly-coated retriever.

Labrador Retriever

Far and away the most popular retriever in North America today is the Labrador. These handsome animals have good noses, are strong, are adapted to general work with a gun, are superior in the water, and are very hardy and

Good retrievers must have stamina and great strength, particularly for fetching big, heavy geese. Here, a black Lab retrieves a large honker from a Maryland slough. (*Rick Methot*)

A Labrador retriever delivers a mallard to her master's hand. This breed of dog is handsome, intelligent, enthusiastic, and easily trained.

persevering in retrieving any waterfowl. The Labrador's coat is dense. Beneath the coat the animal is compactly built. A dog given good conditioning possesses tremendous strength both for hunting on land and for swimming long distances.

Besides its excellence as a water dog, the Labrador's great popularity can be attributed to several other reasons. First, it is exceptionally eager to please and very intelligent. Second, most Labradors are friendly and can become good family dogs as well as waterfowl dogs. Third, they are splendid dogs for hunting such upland game as pheasants, rabbits, and partridges.

Although most Labrador retrievers are glistening black, breed standards permit two other colors—chocolate and yellow. Here, a yellow Lab dashes into a shallow pothole to fetch a mallard.

Chesapeake Bay Retriever

The Chesapeake Bay retriever, which may weigh anywhere from fifty to eighty pounds, is a powerful dog able to cope with virtually any condition of water or elements. At one time it was easily the most popular of all American retrievers. The dog's coarse double coat is a tawny brown, or rather the color of dead reeds and grasses in autumn. This blends neatly with the average duck blind and helps hide the dog from keen waterfowl eyes.

Chesapeakes have been known to swim uninterrupted for as long as thirty minutes in near-freezing water in pursuit of crippled ducks.

A Chesapeake Bay retriever leaps into the water to capture an injured goose before it can escape. "Chessies" aren't as popular as they once were, and they have occasionally been accused of being surly and hard headed. Many of us who have hunted with Chesapeakes believe that inappropriate training was to blame. With rare exceptions, Chessies tend to be good companions and powerful, determined retrievers. (*Gaines Dog Research Center*)

Even after this ordeal the dogs suffered no ill effects and would return to the water on command. Perhaps the main reason the Chesapeake is no longer the most popular waterfowl retriever is that a few individuals have developed surly dispositions and are not always easy to train. At least, that is the impression many gunners have.

American Water Spaniel

Only two breeds of dogs are recognized as being of American origin, and one of these is the handsome American water spaniel. Long familiar to sportsmen, it has not been popular in recent years for reasons hard to explain. The dog swims naturally and with considerable stamina. It is medium in size, rather short in the legs, sturdy, of typical spaniel character, has a curly coat, and over all is an active, muscular dog. Its disposition is very amiable, and most water spaniel owners consider it a dog of great intelligence.

Golden Retriever

A breed of growing popularity is the golden retriever. Goldens are strikingly handsome dogs, very powerful, and of good disposition. It is my own experience, at least, that they are not as determined in pursuing crippled waterfowl as are Labs. Of course, there are countless exceptions to this, but I am speaking of the average golden retriever versus the average Labrador.

Irish Water Spaniel

The Irish water spaniel is a product of the west coast of Ireland, where hunting waterfowl in the numerous bogs and marshes is an important and unique sport. Perhaps no water dog, unless it would the Chesapeake, has a coat better adapted for the icy conditions of a typical waterfowling day. This spaniel's general appearance is that of a huge, shaggy, liver-colored dog with a ratlike tail. Most Irish water spaniels are good watchdogs, aloof yet still very companionable with close friends.

The golden retriever is big, strong, and a good swimmer. In recent years this breed has been growing in popularity.

Springer Spaniel

The springer spaniel is a good swimmer and can be used to great advantage as a waterfowl retriever. However, it is even better as a flushing and retrieving dog in the uplands, and most springers are used only on rare occasions when upland-hunting masters go duck hunting.

Neither the curly-coated nor the flat-coated retriever is very well known or very popular in the United States today. However, they are highly capable dogs and make valuable companions on any duck-hunting expedition.

Training and Feeding

It is a rare retriever of good breeding that does not take naturally to its work. In other words, teaching a retriever to retrieve is seldom a difficult task. Training is a very pleasant pastime

and can furnish a duck hunter many pleasant hours of recreation during the off-season.

A most important point in retriever training is basic instruction in obedience. An obstreperous or undisciplined dog cannot be tolerated in a boat or blind. A retriever should be taught to lie down and to stay down quietly when commanded to do so. It must never become restless or a nuisance. It is also necessary that a retriever respond to the command "heel." When jump-shooting or sneaking up on ponds on hands and knees, the dog should hunker down and follow just behind or just beside the hunter. In any other case, it will flush the ducks long before a hunter can reach close enough shooting range.

There is an alternative to teaching a dog yourself and that is to employ a professional trainer. But the most important thing, whether the dog is trained at home or by a professional, is to give your dog plenty of exercise and experience.

There are many good volumes about retriever training, and it is a very good idea to obtain one of these while your retriever is still a puppy. Another good idea is to consult with other sportsmen who have successfully trained retrievers for the field. Still another bit of good advice is to join one of the retriever clubs that now exist in almost every community in the country.

For a great many years, various associations of gun dog owners, trainers, and breeders have organized and conducted field trials, and many of the competing dogs have become renowned national champions. These contests and the activities surrounding them have been of great value in the breeding and training of retrievers as well as other types of hunting dogs. However, field trials can be very time consuming, and for the average waterfowler they may be unsatisfactory in other ways. For one thing, the very nature of traditional trials dictates somewhat artificial situations and conditions. For another, the emphasis on a dog's working style and on class, regional, and national competition may not always be in the best interest of an ordinary dog-owning hunter. Although some dogs are outstanding in both trials and actual hunting, others are not. Some, oddly enough, shine at trials but seem less comfortable in the real hunting world.

For these reasons, a number of *hunting* (as opposed to traditional field trial) groups of re-

Every year, waterfowlers bring down but fail to recover a great many birds. The percentage of lost cripples is a disgrace we cannot afford in an age of diminished habitat and proportionally reduced wildlife populations. A rugged, aggressive retrieving dog like this one—well trained to follow hand signals as well as voice or whistle signals—substantially reduces losses and is therefore one of the waterfowler's personal conservation assets.

triever owners and trainers have been founded. While they conduct trials, these tend to be somewhat less formal than the traditional ones, and there's no great pressure on members to compete. They also hold less competitive "tests" in order to rate a dog's progress or level of development—and they organize practice and instructional sessions, seminars, and clinics which most retriever owners find enormously worthwhile.

Even if you've had (or expect to have) no trouble at all in turning a pup or a grown dog into an ideal retriever, you may want to obtain information on tests, training, and other activities from one of the following organizations:

Hunting Retriever Club, Inc.
100 E. Kilgore Rd.
Kalamazoo, MI 49001-5598

North American Hunting
Retriever Association
P.O. Box 154
Swanton, VT 05488

American Kennel Club
Hunting Retriever Tests
51 Madison Ave.
New York, NY 10010

Some waterfowlers own one of the Continental breeds often called "utility dogs" or "versatile hunting dogs"—such as the German shorthaired pointer, German wirehaired pointer, wirehaired pointing griffon, Brittany spaniel, or even the Pudelpointer. If you use one of these breeds for hunting, another organization can help you in polishing your dog's performance. It's the North American Versatile Hunting Dog Association, whose local chapters conduct periodic training clinics and demonstrations. You'll be welcome even if you use your dog only for fetching ducks and not for upland hunting (though there's no reason to limit a utility dog's work to waterfowling) and you'll enjoy the clinics whether you're inexperienced or an old hand with gun dogs. For information, send a stamped, self-addressed envelope to John F. O'Brien, NAVHDA, 4302 Rt. 21, Marion, NY 14505.

No retriever is any better than its physical condition. A poorly conditioned dog cannot swim the long distances that are often necessary. Besides physical conditioning before opening day, a dog's diet becomes an extremely important factor. Correct feeding is particularly important among such large breeds as retrievers. And that is doubly true during their maturation period. Most of these dogs weigh only a pound or two at birth, but in another year they may grow to eighty or ninety pounds.

Because retrievers grow so fast, attention should be given to proper diet. Generally, a young retriever's diet should be fortified with vitamins and minerals. You should consult your veterinarian about these supplements and about diet in general.

Although Labs, Chessies, and goldens are the most commonly used retrievers, several other breeds are extremely adept "water dogs." Properly trained springer spaniels, for example, are as skillful on the marshes as in the uplands. Here, a trainer works to "steady" a fine springer before tossing a retrieving dummy. (*Leonard Lee Rue III*)

Many retriever owners are constantly in doubt about how much to feed their dogs. There is no correct answer to cover all situations. Most commercial dog foods are the result of much research and they provide fairly complete and well-balanced diets. For commercial foods, here are a few rules of thumb that can be used as a basis in feeding an active retriever. For young retrievers (until they're at least a year old) figure about one ounce of wet meal or canned food per pound of body weight per day. For older animals, figure one half to three fourths of an ounce per pound of body weight each day.

If you prefer dry meal, figure one and a half to two pounds of dry meal per day per thirty-five pounds of dog. All these figures may be increased slightly during those busy periods in autumn when the dogs are frequently working in the field. During other periods, when the dogs are largely idle, the rations can be cut slightly. But remember that these are only rough guidelines. Ask your veterinarian what's best for your particular dog.

Of course, your dog should be immunized against distemper, rabies, and other diseases common among dogs. During the warm months, the dog should probably be given a daily heartworm preventive, which is available in tablets that seem to be very agreeable to the canine palate.

CHAPTER 11

THE WATERFOWLER'S EQUIPMENT

As any experienced waterfowler knows, duck and goose hunting can be a cold business. A good part of waterfowling means sitting in a blind, and modern thermal underwear and insulated outer clothing are excellent for this. However, such an outfit can actually become too warm when you're slogging through marshes.

Ideal Waterfowler's Clothing

The ideal hunting outfit for a very cold day in a blind is a set of insulated underwear over which woolen pants and shirt are worn. I also like to wear a soft woolen dickey or turtleneck sweater under my shirt. On the coldest days a quilted down jacket or one insulated with a synthetic is ideal. On other days a standard duck-hunting jacket is fine, and the older and more weathered it is, the better. For headgear the fur-lined or insulated hats with earflaps are just about perfect.

Of course, waterfowling may also be done in warmer climates and on bluebird days. In these situations a hunter will simply have to follow his own preference to meet local conditions. But if he is wise, he will always be prepared for the worst, because among other things, autumn weather is extremely changeable and uncertain.

The last decade or so has been marked by the welcome introduction of light, thin, efficient synthetic insulating materials such as Thermolite and Thinsulate, waterproofing laminations such as Gore-Tex, synthetically improved fabrics, reliable reversible zippers (which can be zipped from the top or bottom or either side of a reversible garment), Velcro closures, and enormous advances in the design of hunting clothes. A good modern parka, for instance, is likely to have a comfortable, easily detachable hood; perhaps a flap to protect your lower face; easily accessible pockets with room enough for shells, sandwiches, and heaven knows what else; cuffs and a collar that really will block out snow, rain, and ice; sometimes a large game pocket, and sometimes even a waterproof flap at the rear that can be lowered so you can sit on a wet surface and maintain a dry bottom.

Some brands of hunting clothing also feature optional systems of zip-in/zip-out liners and shells that can be worn separately or together. If midmorning turns wet and warm, you might remove the inner vest and insulating liner and just wear the outer, waterproof shell. If it turns hot and dry, you might just wear the vest. During very cold weather, you wear all the components and they still won't bind you. The sleeves, shoulders, and body of such a parka are designed for freedom of movement, so your arms won't be hampered as you swing your gun smoothly ahead of a duck. Hunters have always worn "layered" clothing, to be peeled off like the outer layers of an onion or put back on as needed. But clothing designed specifically for this purpose has been a big improvement. Columbia Sportswear, a pioneering manufacturer in this field, labeled this type of design the Interchange System, and it's an apt name.

All the major brands of hunting parkas, jackets, vests, hats, gloves, pants, coveralls, and so on can be bought in camouflage patterns (and

Here's what a well-dressed lady waterfowler might wear for an early season, warm-weather outing in watery habitat. Peggy Bauer (the author's wife) is wearing hip boots and a light camouflage jacket with ample flap-pocket room for snacks, small items of equipment, and spare ammunition (handy and secure in elastic shell-holder loops inside two of the pockets).

Waterfowlers have long exploited the concept of "onion-layering" their clothing for quick changes in accordance with the vagaries of the day's weather. The modular zip-in/zip-out liner designs of many modern parkas and other hunting garments make the procedure much more convenient and efficient. This example is the Columbia Sportswear camo-fleece field vest and outer jacket.

most also come in drab, solid colors). In fact, some companies offer a wide choice of camo-patterns to blend with marsh backgrounds, woodlands, early or late season, leafy or grassy vegetation, or the bark of trees. Waterfowl can distinguish colors at great distances, and are quick to take alarm if they see something that looks wrong in a natural setting—a blaze-orange upland hunting cap is an obvious example. And since you can buy most waterfowling clothes in a camouflage pattern at no extra cost, you might as well do so.

However, I suspect that all the claims and counterclaims about various camouflage colors

and patterns—and the emphasis on camouflage patterns in general—has been based more on fashion and persuasive advertising than on necessity. If you have a favorite old hunting coat in a traditional drab color, don't let anyone tell you that you'll bag a lot more ducks by replacing it with a costly new camo-pattern parka. Unexpected motion probably scares and flares more ducks faster than a color that doesn't quite match its surroundings, so it's important to keep still in the blind until the birds are in range. They can also be alarmed by bright objects that twinkle or reflect the sun. Some hunters who need eyeglasses therefore wear contact

Cold weather and waterfowling go together during much of the season. Today's popular camo-pattern parkas and caps comfort the hunter by means of lightweight but highly effective insulating materials, extremely durable, tear-resistant fabrics, waterproof laminations that retain "breathability" so that the wearer's perspiration is "wicked" away, and back/shoulder/sleeve designs that permit freedom of movement for smooth gun-swinging. Hunter Tom Elman is pictured here in utter comfort on a frigid day. (*Robert Elman*)

For slogging through salt marshes in quest of coastal snow geese, recommended apparel includes chest-high insulated waders, a camouflage-pattern cap with pull-down brim or flaps for ear and neck protection, and a light, warm camo jacket or parka. Note that this gunner's camouflage extends to the finish on his gun. In recent years, camouflaged waterfowl guns have become increasingly popular. (*Rick Methot*)

The concept of layering even extends to waterfowling gloves and mittens. They're modern versions of the military gloves (woolen inner gloves under removable leather shells) used in World War II. Today, however, the shells feature state-of-the-art insulation and the liner gloves may combine several materials. (*Courtesy of Columbia Sportswear*)

lenses. But that isn't really necessary if you shade your upper face by wearing a billed cap or brimmed hat.

During a long vigil in a cold blind there is nothing more welcome than a hot beverage and perhaps a hot snack. If a warm clubhouse is nearby, this isn't so important. But if no clubhouse exists or if it is far away, it is a good idea to carry a vacuum container of hot coffee or tea, soup, or hot chocolate. Keep in mind that soup or hot chocolate gives energy faster and in greater volume than coffee or tea. Many hunters like to carry along a can or two of soup and a small stove to heat it.

Most duck hunting requires either hip boots or waders. Which of these the hunter obtains depends more or less upon the situations he will face. Sometimes I have suffered discomfort all through a day because cold water came over the top of my hip boots while I was retrieving a bird or putting out decoys. On the other hand, I have labored unnecessarily across soggy cornfields while wearing waders that I didn't need. It's a matter of preference and need. However, it's a good idea to consider the insulated models no matter which type of gear is selected.

Waterfowlers are not as gadget conscious as some other outdoorsmen. But there are several items of equipment that can make any hunt more pleasant. A good example would be a small camp heater, which can help keep you warm in a blind. Hand warmers are handy to stuff inside pockets, and it's a good idea to carry along a small cushion to sit on. I also carry along two or three pairs of gloves, which can be changed if one or more pairs get wet during the course of hunting.

Boats

Many waterfowling situations require a boat to transport the hunter out to his blind or shooting area. One type of traditional boat still in use is the double-ended punt boat. Actually, the old wooden punt boats are more traditional than useful. They were designed in the days before aluminum and they are unwieldy, especially in the predawn darkness when duck hunters so often set out for their binds.

Many veteran duck hunters will not agree with this, but I believe the most versatile, de-

In the past couple of decades, small fiberglass dinghies have come into increasing use in areas blessed with numerous creeks, small ponds, and potholes—particularly on public hunting grounds. A duck boat of this kind has room for one gunner, his dog, decoys, gun, ammunition, and food, but not much else.

On waters where a hunter must cover a considerable distance to reach his blind, a sturdy aluminum skiff or johnboat is very serviceable and, depending on size, can be trailered or cartopped to the launch. Lightness and durability are big advantages of aluminum. Be sure to select a boat that's rated for a motor of adequate horsepower for safe, easy launch-to-blind commuting. (*Joe Richard*)

Among boats for small, calm waters, the ultimate in portability may be collapsible dinghies such as the Porta-Bote, which actually folds up to a thickness of four inches flat, for cartopping.

pendable, and durable duck boat for most situations is the very shallow-draft, light-aluminum johnboat. This can be rowed, pulled, punted, or paddled wherever there is enough water to float it—and it doesn't need very much water. Of course, it should be painted a dull brown or olive because unpainted aluminum can cause ducks to spook.

There are a great many other kinds of duck boats, old and new, large and small. There are open bays, offshore islands, and other gunning sites along our coasts, on the Great Lakes, and in other regions where waterfowlers use Boston Whalers, large dories, and other craft generally associated with fishing.

The venerable Barnegat sneakbox, one of the oldest and most famous of duck-boat designs, is still in use on big bays. A few of the sneakboxes are still being made of wood and by hand. I've also seen a couple of modern fiberglass-hulled counterparts. These are seaworthy boats that can be run on motors but also have a raisable mast for a sail, and they feature a low pro-

Here's a modern version of the layout boat, which is still in use on the Great Lakes and other large bodies of water. Actually, it's more of a floating blind than a true boat and is usually carried or towed to the gunning site by a tender boat. At top, it's being launched from a small front-console outboard craft. At center, it's anchored amid the decoy spread. The gunner lies almost flat on his back with the gun resting in front of him, on the cockpit edge and foredeck. At bottom, he does a very fast sit-up to get his gun on incoming birds.

Combining easy trailering and storage with spacious-
ness, this unusual version of a square-ended johnboat
hinges amidships to fold up, clamshell-style. When
closed, it's an equipment carrier. This one, called the
Water Snake, is a 170-pound 14-footer (when open) with
a carrying capacity of more than 650 pounds. (*Joann
Kirk*)

Low-profile duckboats of this sort can comfortably carry
two gunners, a dog, guns, and gear. The pictured boat
is designed to plane over the water efficiently with a
small outboard motor running at moderate speed, so it
can get a hunting party out to a blind or back to the
launch quickly. (*Joann Kirk*)

This very small craft accommodates a small, light outboard motor, is easily trailered, and has an extremely
low profile for use with a canopy-type portable blind. If
you maneuver it into a thicket of tall aquatic vegetation, it's effectively hidden even without a canopy blind.
(*Joann Kirk*)

file and stability combined with a spacious
cockpit and foredeck for stowing a great many
decoys and gear.

In parts of the South, shallow-draft pirogues
are in use, as are wider, shallow-draft, flat-
bottomed boats with enormous upraised pro-
pellers at the stern to push air instead of water

so that they can skim over a mere weedy film
of water. There are also wheeled, amphibious
duck boats. Up in New England, Merrymeeting
sculls are still seen occasionally. They're pro-
pelled by a sculling oar that projects rearward
from the stern, positioned so that the operator
can lie low as he sculls the low-profile boat into
range of big rafts of ducks; he then rises to shoot
when they take off. Scullboats are also a popular
tradition on the West Coast.

On the Great Lakes and on some other large,
open bodies of water you'll find layout boats,
which aren't easy to maneuver or propel but
can be towed into place by larger tender boats.
A true layout boat is a small, cramped, low-
profile one-man craft that can be positioned in
the midst of a big spread of diving-duck decoys.
With its gunwales just a little above the surface
of the water, it's inconspicuous—and so is the
gunner, who lies flat on his back in it, or nearly
so, until birds fly close enough for a shot. Then
he sits up fast to shoot.

There are some hunters—who obviously are
in good physical condition and impervious to
repeated fast sit-ups—who love layout boats
and shoot very well from them. There are others
who swear that layout boats were invented to
torture and humiliate hunters. When the gunner

This large amphibious craft, shown on Tennessee's Reelfoot Lake, serves as a roomy blind when it reaches its destination. It bears a camouflage paint pattern and its sides are thatched with vegetation. (*Don Kirk*)

in a layout has filled his limit or taken a given number of shots, the tender pulls alongside and he relinquishes his place to another gunner who may be equally adept at the technique or equally masochistic.

In addition to these traditional boats there are assorted newer types, most of them made of molded fiberglass, a few of them aluminum, and almost all of them painted olive drab or a similar color. A great many are small dinghies with just room enough for one or possibly two hunters, a dog, guns and shells, and a relatively small number of decoys. But some, of course, are larger and more elaborate. A clever design that showed up not long ago was a small but adequate flat-bottom that is hinged amidships

so it can be folded up like a clamshell and used as a cartop gear carrier.

I've seen another, larger type with an aluminum, camouflage-patterned upper shell that amounts to a built-in blind. Called the Duckbuster Boat, it has a stove, heater, refrigerator, interior lighting, bilge pump, comfortable seats for the hunters, and sliding roof hatches so that gunners can stand up fast in the overhead ports and shoot at incoming birds. There are several versions, from sixteen to twenty feet long, and they're motored to the gunning site by a 40-horsepower outboard.

For waterfowlers who don't have to transport their boats long distances over highways, such boats can be a wonderful luxury. Certainly

Here you have an exterior and interior view of an unusual aluminum design called the Duckbuster Boat, built on a wide-beamed, modified johnboat hull with a draft of only four inches so that it remains mobile in very shallow waters. It comes in 16-, 18-, and 20-foot models rated for outboards up to 40 horsepower. It has a separate compartment for the dog and a unique "nose well" that can hold 80 magnum decoys. You can paint it dull green, but options include a camouflage stenciling pattern—and interior options run the gamut from bilge pump and insulated walls to a gas stove, refrigerator, and television! (*Courtesy of Duckbuster Boats, Des Moines, Iowa*)

they're a far cry from the traditional little dinghy-type duckboats or the welterweight canoes used to float creeks for puddle ducks.

Calls and Calling

Every waterfowler eventually acquires at least a few duck and goose calls. If he learns how to use them properly, they can increase his pleasure and his bag, but poor calling will almost invariably scare ducks off instead of attracting them. A hunter who has not learned to call skillfully is better off remaining silent and depending on his decoys to lure the ducks—or else depending on the artful calling of a proficient companion.

Most duck calls are mouth-operated, and hunters sometimes talk of "blowing" them. Some calls can be blown pretty effectively, but most require the hunter to do something more than blowing, like grunting or talking. Bringing his breath up from deep in his throat or from his diaphragm (more or less like a singer), he really utters syllables into the call. The majority of these calls employ single or double reeds inside a more or less cylindrical "barrel" of wood or plastic. Tone, pitch, and volume can be altered and controlled partly by breath and voice, partly by cupping a hand around the end of the instrument.

Not all "mouth calls" employ a reed. There's also a type known as the "tube call" which has a flexible membrane stretched over the end instead of a standard internal reed. For that matter, not all calls are mouth-operated. The bellows-type call has a pleated, cylindrical rubber barrel that can be expanded and contracted, rather like an accordion without a keyboard. Sound is produced when air is forced in and out by expansion and contraction. You can hold the two ends in your hands, theoretically squeezing and stretching to get the sound you want—but don't. To get the most realistic sounds, hold the call by just one end, in one hand, and swing or shake it. A slow swing downward produces a quack (or a honk if it's a goose call) as the air is forced out slowly. Quickly shaking and vibrating the call produces a chatter, like that of gathering and feeding ducks.

Some hunters buy a bellows call because they have the mistaken impression it will be easier to master than the traditional mouth call. That just isn't so. In the hand of a novice, it emits unnatural squawks and moans. Any type of call requires practice.

There are high-pitched reed-type calls that mimic the wood duck's cheeping and hooting, and others designed as teal or pintail "whistles." For most hunters, these are more difficult

A duck call that employs rubber bellows as the sound chamber. You shake this call to imitate the feeding chuckle of puddle ducks.

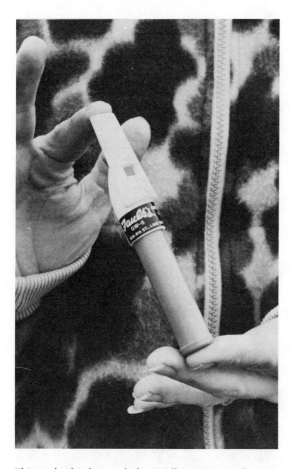

This teal whistle, made by Faulk's Game Calls, is constructed of extremely tough plastic. High-pitched whistling calls of this type also attract baldpates and even pintails—if you learn to blow them realistically. (*Joann Kirk*)

to use realistically than an ordinary mallard-voiced quacking call, although they can be very effective when skillfully used. The fact is, most species of ducks are sufficiently attracted by the sound of a mallard to fly closer and investigate. Moreover, mallards are our most widely distributed ducks. For these reasons, most commercially available calls are intended and "tuned" for mallards.

Yet two mallard calls seldom sound quite alike. Some are louder than others, some more strident, some more flexible in pitch or adaptable to staccato chattering and trilling. Many adept callers hang two different calls around their necks to change sounds quickly in accordance with fast-changing situations. Incidentally, it's wise to put any and all calls on neck lanyards in order to prevent loss and keep them within quick reach.

It's strange but true that a particular style of calling may entice mallards or other species more effectively in one region than another. What works best in Oregon may not be quite as alluring in Alabama. Throughout much of the

This is a typical double-reed call with a hardwood barrel. The hunter's hand on the call's forward end can be used to help control pitch as well as volume. (*Rick Methot*)

Mississippi Flyway, for example, a very common and useful style is called "highballing." A highball is a *very* loud series of quacks designed to draw high-flying ducks down into range. But in most other regions, a coarse, gutteral feeding sound seems to attract ducks more consistently, especially early and late in the day when many flocks are eagerly seeking morning feeding areas and overnight resting areas. (This normal behavior may be reversed, incidentally, when the moon is full or nearly so, because on bright nights ducks and geese often feed nocturnally and rest during much of the day.)

Since the most effective calling varies slightly with region, many hunters depend on trial and error to learn what's best in the areas they hunt. A faster and better way to learn is to hunt with local waterfowlers or guides who have lived and gunned in the area for years. To do that is to "fine-tune" your calling under expert tutelage.

Despite regional variations, the basics remain the same, and variations are quickly learned once the basics are mastered. It must be admitted that some of us just aren't "musically inclined" and never do learn the basics—in which

Here's a small sampling of the many duck and goose calls available. The one at far right is the bellows, or "shaker," type. Next to its handle (upper portion of photo) are teal whistles made in South America. The other calls include whistles and deeper-pitched, single- and double-reed types, some of them factory-made and others handcrafted. The housings, or barrels, are made of materials ranging from impact-resistant plastics to common and exotic hardwoods. (*Joann Kirk*)

case the calling should be left to others. But for most people, skill is acquired in a combination of two ways. The first is to get out in the wetlands as often as possible, listen to the birds, practice imitating them, and gladly accept any tips from experienced callers. The second—a marvelous learning method that wasn't available to our fathers—is to buy a couple of the numerous instructional audiocassettes that are available at sporting goods stores and by mail order. Some of these come with instructional booklets that help, but the most valuable element is the tape itself. Listen to it and practice with it.

When you manage to sound like what you hear, you need to learn one more crucial lesson: when to call and when not to call. As a general rule, call when ducks are far off and you want to attract their attention, and keep calling when

birds seem to lose interest and swing away from you. But when they head toward you, keep quiet. As long as ducks are coming your way, don't call and don't move.

Most gunners feel that geese are easier to imitate than ducks, and there are experts who do so without any mechanical aid, using nothing but their breath and vocal cords—and usually a cupped hand or two in front of their mouth. The Cree guides of the north are famous for this. Most of us, however, use wooden or plastic-barreled reed calls (and some use the tube call or the bellows call). These goose calls are pretty much like the standard duck calls, only larger.

The same rule of restraint in calling applies, but a little more flexibly. Geese sometimes seem to be attracted to your spread of decoys but are approaching somewhat uncertainly or hesitantly. If you're good with a call, you may allay

This photo shows the value of the relatively short barrels on a typical double gun for jump-shooting. Although birds may rise far ahead of you, they may also flush almost from underfoot—like many upland birds. You therefore want a fast-handling gun, and a double like this can swing fast to get on target.

In cold, snowy weather you must have a gun that functions reliably under adverse conditions, and you really don't want one with fancy wood or engraving that tempts you to pamper it or makes you concentrate less on spotting incoming birds than on keeping your shotgun clean, dry, and unscratched.

their fears and coax them in—if you don't overdo it.

In goose calling, as in duck calling, instructional cassettes are an enormous help if you listen and practice frequently. But learning the subtleties of when to call or be silent is best accomplished by sharing a blind with an experienced goose caller.

Guns and Loads

What kind of gun is best for waterfowling? That question cannot be answered definitively because duck and goose shooting involves so many variables. Probably the best advice is to use the kind of scattergun with which you shoot best and feel most comfortable—in all likelihood the same kind you carried afield when learning to shoot or the kind you use to break clay targets or hunt upland game.

If you're relatively inexperienced in the various shooting sports, that advice may not be sufficiently helpful, so I will briefly discuss the features of various shotgun actions. I feel that a single-barreled, single-shot action is an extremely poor choice since you will almost never be able to reload the gun fast enough for a second shot at a departing bird. When I see a gun of that kind in the wetlands, I assume it's the only one the hunter owns and right now he just can't afford to buy something better. The real choice, then, is among the following action types: pump-action repeaters, semiautomatic repeaters, bolt-action repeaters, and double-barreled guns (either side-by-side models or over/unders).

The oldest type is, of course, the double with side-by-side barrels. If you're a very proficient wingshot and don't attempt to bring down birds that are beyond reasonable range, you will seldom need a third shot. (If you're like most of us, you'll be gleeful any time you manage to bring down one or two birds with two shots before the ducks or geese have flared out of range.) If you're not very proficient, however, you may frequently need a third fast shot, so the double would not be for you. The side-by-side double is the handsomest and trimmest of hunting guns, and is beautifully balanced for smooth handling.

Most over/under guns are comparably well balanced, though deeper in profile since one barrel is situated below the other. Some gunners feel that an over/under is also a trifle slower to reload than a side-by-side, since the action must be opened wider to expose the breech end of the lower barrel fully enough for ejection of the fired shell and insertion of a fresh one. The difference is so minimal that I regard it as totally insignificant. A much more important consideration is whether you shoot better when you align your eye along the narrow sighting plane of the over/under or along the rib flanked by a barrel on each side—a much wider total plane—on a side-by-side gun.

Many waterfowlers shoot better with the side-by-side, as they've mastered the skill of using the rib alone as a sighting plane (without letting the barrel on each side distract or confuse them) while at the same time they can use the total width of the barrels as a kind of visual guide in judging the lead—forward allowance—needed to hit a fast-flying target. Remember, you must not aim directly at the target as you would with a rifle when shooting at a stationary target. Unless the bird happens to be at eye level and flying directly toward or away from you (a rarity) you must swing the muzzle ahead of the target, maintaining a smooth follow-through until the shot has left the barrel. That's the only way to make the shot pellets and the bird arrive at the same spot at the same instant.

But while many waterfowlers shoot better with a side-by-side, even more of them shoot better with the over/under. The narrow sighting plane helps them track a target and swing through and ahead of it more precisely. If a gunner isn't experienced with one type of gun or both and doesn't have any idea which would serve him best, the over/under is probably the safest bet.

At one time, the great advantage of a typical single-barreled repeater (whether it happened to be a pump or an auto) was the capability of firing five or even more fast shots without reloading. That may still be of some limited advantage in certain kinds of upland hunting, but waterfowling is another matter. Most (not all) pumps and autos have a five-shot capacity, but when used for waterfowling the magazine must be plugged to conform with federal and state regulations; that is, the magazine must hold

Browning BSS Standard Grade side-by-side.

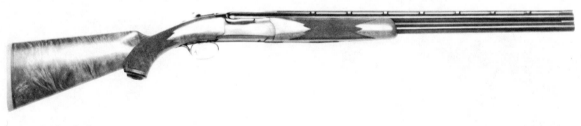

Winchester Model 23 side-by-side with interchangeable screw-in Winchokes.

Diarm 10-gauge magnum Waterfowl Special side-by-side, imported from Spain.

Ruger Red Label over/under.

Winchester Waterfowl Model 101 over/under with Internal Winchoke tubes.

Beeman/Fabarm Gamma Model over/under.

Browning Citori over/under with optional screw-in Invector choke tubes.

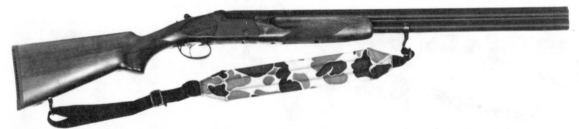

American Arms/Diarm Waterfowl Special over/under.

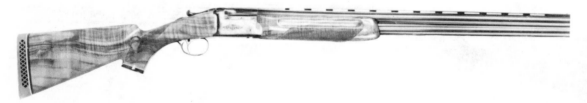

Weatherby Orion over/under.

Remington Model 870 Wingmaster Special Purpose Magnum pump with interchangeable Rem Choke tubes.

Mossberg/Smith & Wesson Model 3000 Waterfowler pump.

Mossberg Model 500 pump with interchangeable Accu-Choke tubes.

Browning BPS pump with optional Invector choke tubes.

Weatherby Model 92 pump with Integral Multi-Choke tubes.

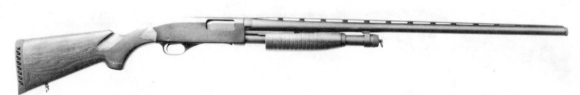

Winchester Waterfowl Model 1300 pump with Winchoke tubes.

Ithaca Camo Seal Mag 10 autoloader with camo-pattern Teflon coating from butt to muzzle.

Mossberg/S&W Super Waterfowler Model 1000 autoloader with camo finish and synthetic "Speedloading" shell-holder stock.

Browning Auto-5 Magnum 12 with optional Invector choke tubes.

Remington Model 11-87 Special Purpose Magnum autoloader with Rem Choke tubes.

Winchester Ranger autoloader (economy edition of Winchester Model 1500).

Weatherby Model 82 autoloader with Integral Multi-Choke.

only two shells so that with a cartridge in the chamber it will fire no more than three shots without reloading.

That limit on capacity has been in effect for many decades and probably will never be changed. Moreover, in some states your shotgun cannot legally hold more than three shots even if you're hunting upland game rather than waterfowl. That's why repeaters come with plugs inside the magazine. The plugs are removable, but many hunters leave them in the magazine at all times (except when disassembling a gun for a thorough cleaning. All the same, three quick shots are of benefit to many gunners, and they are apt to choose a pump or auto rather than a double-barreled gun.

The pump-action has long been the favorite among American waterfowlers, and this popularity has several sources. For a great many years, the simple, massive, ruggedly built mechanism of the pump gun was more reliable and durable under adverse conditions than an auto. Not even salt spray and the infiltration of grit, seeds, and traces of mud would be likely to cause a serious malfunction of the action (a plugged barrel, that most dangerous of all firearm hazards, is another matter). A semiautomatic, or autoloader, would sometimes suffer a malfunction under harsh waterfowling treatment, but with the better modern autoloaders this is no longer much of a concern.

A second reason for the pump gun's popularity has been that such guns are and always were made in a wide variety of models and grades, from expensive and beautiful to plain and cheap. Smart shopping could get you a plain, cheap one that shot just as well as more expensive guns.

A third reason was that a pump would function smoothly with a wide spectrum of loads, from light field and skeet ammunition to heavy, extra-powerful loads. An auto employs the energy (most often in the form of gas, but in some models in the form of barrel recoil) of each fired shot to cycle the action for the next shot. The amount of energy has to be precisely right. A lot of old-time autos could therefore handle only a limited variety of loads or else had to be taken down so that a piston ring or other device could be adjusted before switching to heavier or lighter loads.

In recent years, however, many autoloading systems have been redesigned. You can now buy a semiautomatic shotgun that will handle a wide spectrum of ammunition, from puny to hefty loads, reliably and without any special adjustment. This is one reason autoloaders have been gaining in popularity. Another advantage of the autoloading system is that the recoil felt by the shooter is slightly reduced since some of the energy generated by firing is "bled off" to cycle the action. Actually, the difference is so slight that I doubt if most shooters notice it. In the excitement of trying to shoot fast at flying birds, few of us ever notice the recoil of a shotgun, regardless of its type of action.

Some gunners also prefer an auto because of its speed of fire. Everything except pulling the trigger is done automatically and mechanically; that is, the fired shell is ejected, a fresh shell is fed from the magazine into the chamber, and the gun is cocked and locked without the need of any manual movement. The gun will fire its second and third shot as fast as you can pull the trigger. With a pump, you must use your forward hand to pull the pump handle rearward and then push it forward again to accomplish those same steps. All the same, the highly touted speed of fire of an auto is largely theoretical—or at least academic. With practice, a pump-gunner can fire his "trombone-action" scattergun just about as fast as the auto-gunner. That brings me back to my original premise: you'll do best with the action you're most accustomed to or feel most comfortable with.

Pumps and autos are longer than double-barreled guns, since they require more receiver length to contain their repeating actions. They are also relatively deep in configuration since they employ a tubular magazine below the barrel. They are not quite as well balanced as a good double, but they do provide extra shots.

At one time, single-barreled repeaters offered another advantage—a variable choking device. The two most widely used types were the Cutts and the Poly-Choke. The Cutts, a rather long barrel extension fitted to the muzzle, accommodated interchangeable choke tubes, while the Poly was a shorter, slightly bulbous extension with a knurled ring that could be turned from one choke setting to another. Thus the hunter could have any muzzle constriction, from true cylinder (no choke at all) to full or even extra-full choke.

The tighter the choke is, of course, the tighter will be the pattern of pellets. This can be an advantage at long range, as in pass-shooting, since the patterns open up (and quite a few pellets fall away) as the "shot string" travels. A wider, more "open" pattern, on the other hand, is far better on moving targets at short range because at least some of the pellets in a wide pattern are likely to hit the target. For many years, shooting authorities have tried to persuade sportsmen that a major reason for misses and for injuring rather than cleanly killing birds is the tendency to use "too much choke."

Because of the rib that joins the barrels of double-barreled guns, the old variable-choke devices could not be installed on doubles. Thus, the shooter had a selection of only two chokes—one in each barrel. He could get extra, interchangeable sets of barrels, but they were expensive and it wasn't practical to carry and switch them in the field.

Those old variable chokes are still seen on a good many guns, but they have been pretty well eclipsed by today's interchangeable sets of small screw-in choke tubes which can be very quickly inserted and secured in the muzzle. The older devices were somewhat unsightly. The screw-in tubes are nearly invisible. The modern tubes, whose development was pioneered by Winchester, were at first applicable only to single-barreled guns (either single-shots or repeaters), again because of the rib on doubles and also because of the relatively thin barrel walls on doubles, which weren't suitable for screw-threading. Experimentation and engineering innovations ensued at several manufacturing plants and a number of custom gunsmithing shops. As a result, most guns of every action type can now be purchased with screw-in choke tubes either as standard equipment or options. That particular advantage of the single-barreled repeater is no more.

There is little to say in favor of the bolt-action repeating shotgun. Very few are manufactured, and I don't know of any that come with screw-in tubes, though they do come with the older variable-choke extensions. Evidently, the demand for bolt-action shotguns isn't great enough to justify a change. A bolt-sction shotgun has a box magazine and a total capacity of three shots. It's operated just like a bolt-action rifle. After firing, the spent shell is ejected, a new one is fed into the chamber, and the action is cocked and locked by turning the bolt up, pulling it rearward, pushing it forward and down again into locked position. You get three shots, but nowhere near as quickly as with a pump or auto. Because shotshells are so much larger in diameter than rifle cartridges, the magazine and action area of a bolt-action shotgun is deep and massive. Compared to other scatterguns, such a gun is fat, cumbersome, homely, ill-balanced, and unwieldy. For several reasons it's rather a good choice for turkey hunting, but that is hardly the subject of this book. A few waterfowlers still swear by bolt-action shotguns—perhaps because they've always used bolt-actions, perhaps because bolt-action shotguns are relatively inexpensive.

There are a few hidebound waterfowlers who insist on another supposed bolt-action advantage—an extra-long barrel, which is alleged to steady a gunner's swing for long-range pass-shooting and to add effective range to the load. It does not add effective range because all of the powder is burned before the pellets reach the muzzle. Owing to friction in the barrel, it may, in fact, slightly decrease long-range efficiency. Whether its muzzle heaviness improves the gunner's swing is debatable. In any event, many bolt-action shotguns have come to be known as "Long Toms." Traditionally, waterfowling guns, like trap guns, have had 30-inch barrels—longer than those on upland hunting guns and skeet guns. Some bolt-actions have barrels of 32 inches and even more. The length is simply of no value.

The trend today is toward shorter barrels for waterfowling—28 inches having become a common length—and more open chokes. In part, this is because steel shot tends to pattern tightly. A steel-shot pattern fired from a modified choke may be comparable to a lead-pellet pattern fired from a full choke.

This brings us to the subject of loads—and of steel shot. Few of today's young waterfowlers are aware that as long ago as 1930 studies by game biologists indicated that too many waterfowl (and a few other birds) were being lethally poisoned by the ingestion of spent lead shot. The results of one such study were reported by the More Game Birds in America Foundation—a forerunner of Ducks Unlimited—in 1931. Birds use the muscular action of their gizzards

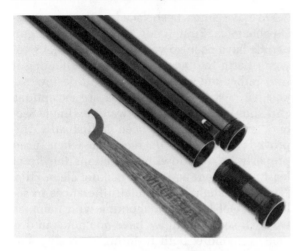

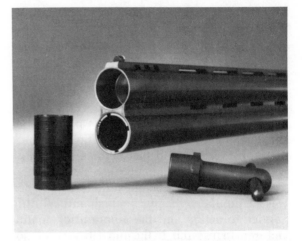

Winchester experimented with screw-in choke tubes in the late 1950s and early 1960s, but the idea was ahead of its time. Pictured here is an updated but transitional version called Winchoke, which gained almost instant popularity in the early 1980s. The photo shows the muzzles of a Model 23 (the world's first side-by-side double featuring screw-in chokes) with the Winchoke removed from one barrel. In the foreground is a small wooden-handled wrench for quick tube installation or removal.

Remington quickly followed Winchester's introduction of screw-in choke tubes by unveiling the Rem Choke system, which is more streamlined than the original Winchoke. As shown in this cutaway view, a Rem Choke tube ends flush with the muzzle—with no visible protrusion. Instead of an external ring to engage the installation wrench, it has recessed notches that engage studs on a small wrench.

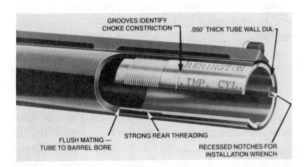

In the mid-1980s, Winchester redesigned its screw-in choke tubes to do away with the installation ring that protruded slightly from the gun's muzzle or muzzles. This is the Internal Winchoke, notched at the front end like Remington's to accept the studs of a small installation wrench.

Several gun manufacturers began to offer invisible or nearly invisible screw-in choke tubes during the mid- and late 1980s. Shown here is the Weatherby version, called IMC, or Integral Multi-Choke. Like the Winchester and Remington devices, the notched tubes are seated all the way into the muzzle by a small studded wrench.

Marlin Model 55 Goose Gun bolt-action with 36-inch full-choke barrel.

to grind their food and make digestion possible. But the muscle alone doesn't do it. Birds "pick grit"—they eat small pebbles and other hard objects, which are used as grinding stones inside the gizzard. Lead-shot pellets, ideal for this purpose and therefore attractive to birds, are extremely poisonous. When a shot is fired, even if the game is bagged, most of the pellets miss and fall to earth or into water. The birds pick them off the land and the bottoms of shallow waters and they sicken and die.

Many years passed before sufficient evidence was accumulated to spur the Fish and Wildlife Service to action and the ammunition manufacturers to research. In the mid-1970s the major ammunition manufacturers began serious research and development with regard to steel shot because the government—prodded by several conservation organizations as well as a number of antihunting groups—revealed its intention to eventually ban lead-shot pellets in severely affected waterfowling areas.

We—the waterfowlers who had the most at stake in the future of the birds—fought the introduction of nontoxic shot with a disgraceful vengeance. Our main reason was that only one basic substitute for lead had been found to be practical. This was so-called steel shot—various soft iron alloys.

Some of the early steel shot was too hard— and gun barrels were too soft—for use without damaging a gun. Buffering materials and plastic wad columns incorporating shot cups or pouches to shield the gun bore from the steel pellets were already available but at that time needed considerable improvement.

Even more important to many of us was the ballistic inferiority of lightweight steel compared to heavy lead. Steel leaves the barrel at higher velocity but loses its speed much sooner than lead. This caused misses and, more to the point, "light hits" that resulted in injured, escaped, unrecoverable birds. A "cripple" might come down half a mile away, to die a slow death or be eaten by a raccoon or stray cat. The loss of cripples was claimed to be greater than the potential wildlife loss through lead poisoning. At first, that might well have been true. (All the studies contradicted one another, but there was no doubt at all that early steel loads were abominable.)

We have since been faced with three inescapable facts. First, today's steel loads and gun barrels have been so vastly improved that steel won't harm the bore unless you're shooting it in a rather old or second-rate gun (a few expensive custom-made doubles are exceptions and shouldn't be used for waterfowling). Second, steel loads have been *ballistically* improved to such a degree that when used properly in waterfowling situations they're at least as efficient as lead in making clean kills. (There are slight but crucial differences in selecting steel loads and shooting with them, as we shall see.) Third, we have no choice in this matter anymore, both in terms of legality and in assuring the future of our waterfowl.

For several years, the U.S. Fish and Wildlife Service headed rather reluctantly along the road toward steel shot. In fairness, it must be said that the Interior Department was formulating its policies and regulations under bewildering pressures; sportsmen opposed steel shot while some conservation groups and antihunting groups opposed lead shot. Eventually, the National Wildlife Federation—a private, nonprofit conservation organization whose state affiliates are composed chiefly of sportsmen—gathered an imposing weight of evidence that lead pellets were killing great numbers of waterfowl and other wildlife that feed on dead or sick waterfowl, including the bald eagle.

Operating in a coalition with other conservation groups, the NWF initiated legal action, which was dropped when the Fish and Wildlife Service finally capitulated, agreeing to phase out lead shot for waterfowling on a nationwide basis by 1991.

So we must now learn to use it properly. It's now available in bore sizes ranging from the little 20 gauge up to the 10-gauge magnum. Steel-shot cartridges are even loaded in the no longer common 16-gauge size. Commercial loads are readily available in 10, 12, and 20 gauge, as are the tools and components for handloading steel-shot cartridges. At the time of this writing, one major ammunition manufacturer offers steel-shot scattergun cartridges in 35 different factory loadings. The array can be bewildering (as can the nomenclature), but a few basic rules and facts will simplify selection.

There will be some argument about this statement, but I do not consider the 20 gauge adequate for most waterfowling. If you have a 20-gauge gun that's chambered for three-inch magnum cartridges, it's suitable for shooting puddle ducks over decoys (provided you're a self-restrained hunter who confines his shots to no more than 35 or 40 yards). Probably the best all-around bore size for waterfowling is 12 gauge, especially if the gun is chambered for 3-inch or 3½-inch magnums. You can then use medium loads for decoying ducks and heavy loads to reach out effectively when you're pass-shooting—and particularly when you're hunting geese.

For a long time, most shooters shied away from the 10 gauge, not only because the guns and shells were all but unavailable but also because of the considerable recoil. But then Ithaca brought out the Mag 10 Auto and rejuvenated the 10-gauge magnum concept, at least to a small degree, for long-range goose shooting. It's a heavy gun, but that's of little consequence when you're sitting in a blind rather than walking the marshes or uplands. And it's weight and semiautomatic action work in concert to dampen perceived recoil somewhat. On the other hand, there aren't many Mag 10 Autos around, and other manufacturers decided against following Ithaca's lead because the uses of such guns are limited. That means a 12-gauge magnum gun remains the best all-around choice, and the 12 gauge chambered for 2¾-inch shells runs a close second.

In 1988, Federal Cartridge Company introduced an ultra-long—3½-inch—12-gauge magnum shell loaded with steel shot, and Mossberg introduced the first gun chambered for it, the pump-action Model 835 Ulti-Mag. "Long" magnum shells must never be fired in a gun chambered only for shorter cartridges, but a chamber that accommodates the longer shells can, of course, safely handle the shorter ones as well. In other words, a gun built for the 3½-inch magnum 12-gauge can also be used with 2¾-inch shells or three-inch magnum shells, making it an extremely versatile shotgun for various kinds of waterfowling, and for other kinds of hunting, too.

When loaded with 1⁹⁄₁₆ ounces of steel shot in a relatively large size such as BB, the Federal 3½-inch 12-gauge shell holds about 24 percent more pellets than the three-inch magnum—only a few less than a 10-gauge magnum. And with today's extremely efficient powders, such a load has a high muzzle velocity, good retained velocity, and excellent penetrating power. This makes it an excellent choice for pass-shooting at large geese, and since a 12-gauge gun chambered for the long shell is both lighter and more versatile than a 10-gauge gun, the 3½-inch 12-gauge shell probably has a long future.

In recent years there has been a trend away from long-barreled guns for waterfowling. If you prefer a 30-inch barrel, that's fine. Personally, I like the 28-inch length, which is all that's really needed even for pass-shooting and which is much handier for the fast swings often demanded in upland hunting. A 28-inch barrel with interchangeable choke tubes gives me an extremely versatile tool that's equally useful for waterfowling and several other kinds of hunting. And it will serve just as well with steel shot as with lead. Because steel shot tends to produce tighter patterns than lead, there has also been a trend away from full choke to less muzzle constriction. A modified choke is best for most waterfowling—a statement that would have been heresy years ago.

As many shooters know, a particular gun usually performs better with some loads than with others. Let's say you have two Winchester Waterfowl Model 1300 pump guns, which appear to be identical. If you spend a couple of hours patterning the two guns with several different loads, you may find that both pumps perform almost identically with each load, or you may find some surprises. Maybe, for example, gun "A" delivers its best (most uniform and dense) patterns at 40 yards with Winchester 2¾-inch loads of No. 6 shot, while gun "B" performs best with comparable Federal or Remington loads.

Or suppose you're trying to decide if you ought to use No. 6 steel pellets in gun "A" for shooting puddle ducks over decoys at a small pond, or if you would be wiser to choose pellets one size larger—No. 4. Theoretically, you don't need No. 4. But comparative patterning experiments may show that one gun delivers better 40-yard patterns with Remington 2¾-inch cartridges charged with 1⅛ ounces of No. 6 pellets,

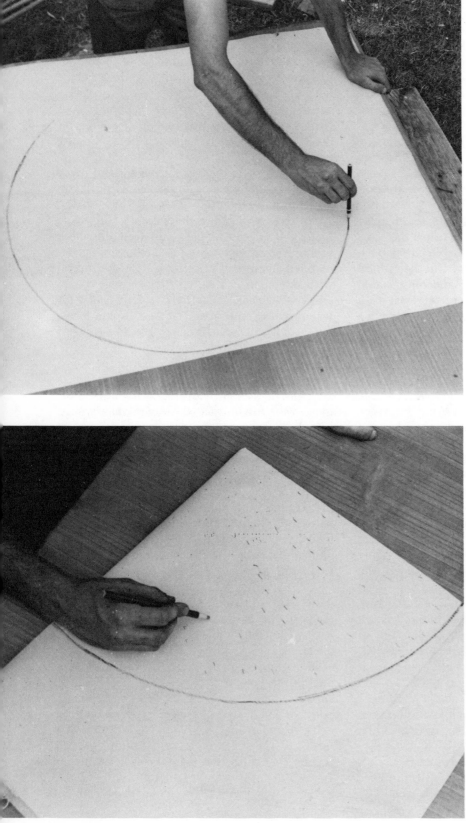

Test patterning various loads in a shotgun is even more important with steel shot than with lead. Patterning sheets can be purchased, but they are very easy and cheap to make for yourself. Stick a tack into the center of a large sheet of heavy paper and attach a pencil or other marker to it with a 15-inch string in order to draw a 30-inch circle. Then simply draw a center mark at which you'll aim. You want to find out how tight, dense, and uniform is the pellet pattern thrown by a given load in your gun. After firing at the sheet, you must therefore mark and count the holes—pellet hits—inside the circle. This job is made considerably faster and easier if you fold the sheet in half and then in half again so you can mark and count the holes in one quarter of the sheet at a time.

while the other gun is significantly more efficient with Remington 2¾-inch cartridges charged with 1⅛ ounces of No. 4 shot. If gun "A" likes No. 4, forget about theory and use the larger shot size.

Such idiosyncrasies have always characterized shotguns, but gun-to-gun differences in patterning with various loads seem to be more pronounced with steel shot than with lead. It's therefore wise to pattern a given gun (or barrel) with the loads you intend to use for a specific kind of waterfowl shooting. The usual method of patterning a gun is to use a commercial or hand-drawn patterning sheet—a paper target with a center mark inside a 30-inch circle. The sheet is secured before a safe backstop, and you then fire a round at it from 40 yards. You inspect it to see what percentage of the cartridge's pellets struck within the circle and whether the pattern of pellet hits within the circle is reasonably uniform. A "blown" pattern (insufficiently uniform and with too many pellets far outside the main concentration) or one with sizable gaps indicates that even if you made a perfect shot at a duck, the bird might fly through the pattern unscathed—or, more likely, the bird would be hit by a pellet or two but not killed. In the latter case, you or your dog would have to chase the cripple down . . . or try to.

Although it's traditional to fire at the 30-inch circle from 40 yards, you'd be well advised to vary that distance in accordance with the kind of waterfowling for which a given load is intended. If you plan to hunt ducks over decoys with No. 4 or No. 6 pellets in a standard or magnum loading, 40-yard patterning makes sense. But if you plan to bag geese in a pass-shooting situation with, say, three-inch magnum loads carrying 1¼ ounces of No. 2 or No. 1 steel shot or even larger pellets, you really want to know if the patterns will do the job at 50 yards. Some gunners pattern various loads at 35, 40, 45, and 50 yards, and occasionally as far as 60 yards.

However, unless you're a truly expert wingshot, I believe you should never shoot at birds beyond 50 or perhaps 55 yards. This is partly because steel is not efficient ballistically at such long range, but it is chiefly because few gunners are expert enough to judge how far to lead a bird at 60 yards. The result of such "sky-busting," as it's called, is far too high a percentage of injured but lost birds.

Steel shot comes in larger sizes than lead shot, and the largest at the time of this writing (designated T, F, and FF shot) have respective pellet diameters of .20, .22, and .23 inch. In other words, F shot is the size of a .22 bullet. Such pellets are generally used in extra-powerful magnum loadings for long-range pass-shooting at large birds—meaning geese. (They're also excellent for turkey hunting under some conditions.) But I don't really believe that most waterfowlers have a legitimate use for shot larger than the BB size (.18 inch) because most of us aren't good enough wingshots to have any excuse for making 60- and 65-yard shots—the intended use for the biggest pellets in the most powerful loads.

Generally speaking, you should use steel pellets one size larger (that is, two numbers larger in standard ammunition designations) than lead pellets for the same purpose. In other words, if you would normally select No. 6 lead for a given hunt, you'd want steel one size larger (No. 4), and if you'd use No. 4 lead you'd go to No. 2 steel. You would also use one size more open choke with steel. If, for a given kind of shooting, you'd select full choke with lead pellets, then you want modified choke for the same purpose with steel. It's not really complicated, but there's admittedly a bit more to it than that—moreover, many of us who have used lead shot in traditional sizes all our lives have difficulty visualizing the sizes and appropriate uses of steel shot. For that reason, you may find it helpful to refer to Appendix I: A Guide to Using Steel Shot.

CHAPTER 12

WILDFOWL COOKERY

Not the least of the dividends of a typical duck hunt is the delicious duck dinner that follows. Many species of waterfowl must rank with the finest of game meats and virtually all of them are good eating if properly prepared. But first there is the matter of plucking and dressing before they are ready for the table.

The sooner it is done, the easier it is to pluck any duck or goose. Plucking a duck immediately after it is shot is not so difficult, but often this isn't convenient to do. In addition, some sportsmen believe that flavor and texture are enhanced if a duck is hung for several days before it is plucked. I do not happen to agree with this theory and believe that ducks should be plucked and dressed no later than the same day they are shot. This is doubly true if any shot has penetrated the intestines or the gall of the duck.

Even if you prefer to hang and "age" your ducks and geese unplucked, there's no reason not to eviscerate them on the day they're shot. You need not remove the feathers to make an incision between the breast and vent so that you can pull out the innards. Furred game of all types—from rabbit to moose—is customarily field-dressed this way, before skinning. The same procedure is recommended for waterfowl and upland birds. I should add that many hunters just don't want to be bothered with plucking, so they skin their birds or simply cut and detach the breast meat. That's a lot faster and less messy than plucking, and with some recipes and cooking methods there's no reason to leave the skin on. With diving and sea ducks, the filleted breast meat is all that really counts. But

most duck and goose dishes are superior if the bird is plucked rather than skinned. The result is worth the time and effort.

Plucking and Dressing

The simplest but not necessarily the easiest way of plucking is to use a thumb and forefinger, picking clumps of feathers and moving against the grain. In other words, from tail to head of the duck. Some shooters first remove the head and tail before they start plucking, but this is a matter of personal preference. I leave the feet on the bird because it gives me a good grip with the hand not used in plucking. If the duck has been dead some time and if water and heat are available, dipping the duck briefly into a bucket of boiling water will be of some slight help in removing the feathers.

A far more convenient method is to bring a pan of water almost to the boiling point, then drop several sticks of paraffin, the same type used in canning jelly and jam, into the boiling water and allow it to melt and form a film on top of the hot water. Five or six standard cakes of paraffin will be enough to dress all of the ducks you are likely to bag in one season. Flaked "plucking paraffin" is occasionally sold at sporting goods stores.

After the paraffin has melted, dip the duck into the bucket until it is entirely covered with a thin coating of wax. Remove, allow the carcass to drain thoroughly, and place the duck aside for a few minutes until the wax stiffens and completely congeals. After the paraffin has cooled, it can be peeled off the duck in virtually the same manner as peeling a tangerine. All but the tiniest pinfeathers come away with it.

A few waterfowlers dip their ducks into a bucket of water to which heaping tablespoons of detergent have been added. This is said to be a superior method for plucking, but I am not sure I would like to have the suds on my meat.

For those who shoot almost every day during the season and thus have a lot of birds to be prepared, electric plucking machines are available. A typical electric plucker utilizes a revolving drum studded with rubber "fingers." It's a small version of the machines used in many commercial poultry operations. With the drum revolving at fairly high speed, you hold the bird against the rubber protrusions, which whip the feathers off. This does the job very quickly, and neatly too if you're careful not to press the bird too hard against the apparatus. Machines of this type are occasionally advertised in waterfowling magazines.

After the duck or goose is plucked, you can remove the head and feet. With a sharp knife make a V-shaped incision just under the breast and toward the vent. Do not cut too deeply or you will puncture the intestine. After you have made this cut, you can reach inside and easily pull out the entrails. It may be necessary to reach inside the cavity with your knife to cut free the trachea and the gullet, which are attached to the body of the bird. Not all hunters believe in washing a duck either inside or out after it has been dressed and drawn. However, my advice is to rinse it thoroughly.

If the birds are to be frozen rather than cooked immediately, it's much better to seal individual ducks or geese in freezer bags. If not sealed in this manner, ducks tend to become dehydrated in a fairly short time.

Any strong taste that exists in ducks, and this has been greatly exaggerated, usually is concentrated in the fat the ducks accumulate under the skin and near the edges of the body cavity. When dressing a duck, no matter whether you use the entire carcass or only the fillets, it is a good idea to trim off all the fat you can reach.

Hanging

All ducks, and especially geese, can be tenderized by aging them for two or three days before cooking. They should be placed where the temperature hovers between thirty-five and forty degrees. At these temperatures, ducks will keep for as long as four or even five days, depending upon how quickly they have been dressed after shooting. Although the aging process is known as "hanging," you can simply age your birds in the refrigerator.

Recipes and Cooking Tips

Many inexperienced waterfowlers (and their spouses) are sorely disappointed with the results of their first attempts to cook ducks or geese, and the reason often is that people assume wild birds are as fatty as their domestic counterparts. If you've roasted store-bought ducks or geese, you've probably put them on a roasting rack (a good idea with any roast meat) and then noticed that vast quantities of melted fat dripped down from the rack to collect in the bottom of the roaster. Chances are, you drained off a pint or more of rendered fat. That's because farm-bred birds don't do much but stand or sit around eating and putting on weight, fat, and cholesterol. Wild birds have to work hard for a living, and still harder during hunting season when they're making their long migratory flights. Wild ducks and geese are lean! And even the little bit of fat you find on them during preparation is trimmed off.

When you roast a fat domestic duck, it's a good bet you puncture the skin in a number of places to let the melting fat emerge and drain off more easily. In the process, the duck pretty well bastes itself. With a typical wild duck or goose, you'd better do the basting—and in many instances that means a lot of basting. Some waterfowl chefs like to lard a bird inside and out before roasting, or simply lay several bacon strips over the meat. You'll just have to use your own judgment about this, because not every wild duck or goose is excessively lean. In fact, early in the season, some wild geese tend to be almost as fatty as domestic geese, so you'll want to cook them for about half an hour, breast down, in an open roaster at 400 or 450 degrees; then pour off the rendered fat and continue roasting them breast up, covered, at about 350 degrees.

No two sportsmen and no two cooks agree on

exactly how ducks should be handled. One school believes that wild ducks should be eaten nearly rare and another school believes that they should be cooked until they are almost overdone. Probably the best method lies somewhere in between, and herewith follow some of the most delicious recipes I have been able to accumulate in many years.

Pressed Mallard. My friend Frank Sayers enjoys cooking ducks as much as he enjoys hunting them. Several times every season he makes a huge production of preparing his special pressed mallard. Waterfowlers who have never tasted this elegant but robust concoction are most unfortunate. Frank roasts four mallards in a 400-degree oven for about twelve minutes, then places them on a wooden carving board. Very neatly he removes the breasts, or rather fillets them, and then sets the rest of the carcasses aside. The carcasses are then placed in a duck press and the liquors and juices are extracted.

Beforehand, two sauces have been prepared in chafing dishes. The first chafing dish contains melted butter blended with currant jelly. To this add a teaspoon of salt, a pinch of cayenne pepper, a tablespoon of Worcestershire sauce, a few drops of Tabasco, and the liquid squeezed from the duck carcasses. Now the breasts of the duck are floated in the chafing dish that contains this sauce.

A second sauce is made by grinding up the duck hearts and livers after they have been sautéed and salt and pepper have been added. The ground-up hearts and livers are then mixed with a minced celery heart, diced onions, and enough dry sherry to make a thick liquid. After the breasts are simmered slowly and thoroughly in the first sauce, they are covered with the second sauce and served. Most people who have tasted Frank's pressed duck say it is too good to be true.

Kelsor Smith's Recipe. This dish was named after its creator, a marvelous chef at Remington Farms, near Chestertown, Maryland.

Place any number of mallards, pintails, or blacks in a pan, breast up. Sprinkle each duck with one tablespoon of cooking sherry. Season each duck with one-half teaspoon of celery salt, one-half teaspoon of onion salt, one-half tea-spoon of celery seed, one-quarter teaspoon of curry, one-half teaspoon of salt, one-quarter teaspoon of pepper. Let the ducks sit in the pan from thirty minutes to an hour.

Now chop one small onion and one stalk of celery and place them in the pan, add a quarter inch to a half inch of water, and bake at 500 degrees until the breasts are brown—this takes about twenty minutes. Turn the ducks over and bake until the backs are brown. Now cover and cook one more hour at 300 degrees. The total cooking time is two hours. If dressing is desired, use any poultry recipe inside the ducks.

Lew Baker's Recipe. Some years ago my hunting friend Lew Baker prepared a brace of canvasbacks and the result was memorable. After carefully cleaning and hanging the canvasbacks for two days, Lew stuffed each one with a quartered onion and a slice of lemon, then filled the cavity with heavily peppered sauerkraut and slices of apple in about equal quantities. After sewing up the birds, Lew rubbed them with flour, salt, and pepper before placing them in a roasting pan.

Next he packed sauerkraut tightly around the birds and added plenty of sauerkraut juice in the bottom of the pan. He sprinkled a tablespoon apiece of granulated sugar on the tops of the birds and then roasted them until brown and very tender. The ducks and sauerkraut were served with coleslaw and cold bottles of ale. If you do not believe this was an extraordinary dinner, just try it sometime.

Broiled or Fried Fillets. The simplest and surely one of the most delicious ways to cook any duck is to broil the fillets over charcoal or to deep-fry them in peanut oil. They can be cooked either rare, medium, or well-done to suit anybody's taste. When broiling the ducks, I usually make a liquor of vinegar, melted butter, and seasoning with which to baste the fillets during cooking.

Duck Stroganoff. There is something about wild ducks that inspires many elaborate recipes. A good example is duck Stroganoff. The ingredients are: three or four ducks from which the meat has been cut into bite-size chunks, salt, pepper, paprika, nutmeg, butter or cooking oil, two medium onions chopped fine, one cup of sour cream, two tablespoons of tomato sauce, and a half pound of mushrooms, either fresh or canned.

After browning the onions in butter, place the duck pieces in the pan to brown, then remove the meat and keep it hot. Brown the mushrooms in the duck juices, return the meat to the skillet, and season it with salt, pepper, paprika, and a liberal sprinkling of nutmeg. Add tomato sauce, more butter or cooking oil if needed, and simmer the whole works for about an hour and a half or until the meat is very tender. Add small amounts of hot water to keep the juices at about a constant level. At the end add half the sour cream and stir. Cook for another ten or fifteen minutes over a very low heat, stir in the remainder of the sour cream and serve immediately over wild rice.

Roast Duck Supreme.   The chef's specialty at a large duck-shooting club on western Lake Erie is called Roast Duck Supreme. Soak any number of large ducks in salt water overnight. After this, salt, pepper, and use celery salt inside the ducks. Place quartered apples, onions, and celery leaves inside the ducks, then cover them with bacon or salt-pork slices and place them in a roaster. Cook the ducks breast up in two inches of consommé or water in a closed roaster in a 350-degree oven for three and a half hours, basting frequently. To pass the time while the ducks are cooking, the chef can prepare the following orange sauce, which some shooters prefer although others do not.

Ingredients for the orange sauce are: a quarter cup of butter, a half teaspoon of salt, one and a half cups of consommé, two tablespoons of currant jelly, a dash of cayenne pepper, the grated rind of one orange, three-quarters cup of orange juice, fresh if possible, one jigger of dry sherry, and a tablespoon of flour. The butter is melted in a double boiler, and the flour, salt, and cayenne pepper are blended in gradually. Next the consommé is added; then orange rind, jelly, and sherry are blended in. The oven is turned up to 400 degrees to brown the ducks, which are brushed with some of the orange juice. They are cooked fifteen minutes more before serving, and the remaining orange sauce is served on the side.

Crisped Teal.   Here is a delicious recipe for teal or wood ducks. It requires very little preparation, very little effort, and few ingredients. The small ducks are cut or split in half, then roasted with the outside of the ducks up for about thirty minutes in a 450-degree oven. Just before removing them from the oven, they can be brushed with melted butter in which a clove or two of garlic has been crushed. When the skin is crisp, the ducks are ready to eat.

Barbecued Coot and Peppered Coot.   Many shooters consider coot inedible, but this isn't true, and herewith I submit two recipes which are well worth any outdoor cook's time and effort.

The first is called barbecued coot. Take any number of coot and cut the breasts and legs into bite-size pieces. Marinate these for about two hours—not longer—in sauterne or dry sherry. Now skewer the pieces alternately with carrots, onions, or other vegetables and bacon. Broil over charcoal, basting frequently with the same marinade liquor.

This next recipe, peppered coot, calls for four birds dressed, skinned, cleaned, and cut for frying. It also requires a half teaspoon of sage, a half teaspoon of freshly ground pepper, one-half cup of flour, two tablespoons of dried or chopped parsley, one large green pepper chopped up, one garlic bud finely chopped, one medium-size onion chopped, and one teaspoon Worcestershire sauce. Cut the meat from the breast and leg bones, removing any fat. Salt to taste. Brown the meat in a Dutch oven in a mixture of bacon fat and butter, after dredging in a mixture of flour, sage, and freshly ground pepper. Fry all the ingredients separately in butter and pour over the meat. Cover and simmer for about two hours, adding water if necessary. The finished product is enough to make any shooter change his mind about coot.

Wild Duck Chinese Style.   Tracy Balcomb, president of the George Weidemann Brewing Company, in Newport, Kentucky, gave me this delicious recipe for wild duck Chinese style. Naturally, one of the ingredients is beer.

The recipe calls for two two-pound wild ducks of any kind, two cloves minced garlic, one tablespoon salt, one-half teaspoon freshly ground pepper, one-quarter cup melted butter, one apple halved, one-quarter cup dry mustard, one-half cup beer, two tablespoons soy sauce, one cup apricot preserves, and one tablespoon lemon juice. Mix to a paste the garlic, salt, and pepper, rub it into the ducks, and brush the breasts heavily with butter. Place half an apple in each duck, and arrange the ducks in a shallow roasting pan, breast up. Roast in a 400-degree oven for fifteen minutes.

Next mix together the mustard, beer, soy sauce, apricot preserves, and lemon juice. Reduce the heat in the oven to 350 degrees, pour the sauce over the duck, and roast thirty minutes longer, basting frequently. It serves four people normally, but is just about right for two duck hunters who are hungry enough to eat a raw goose.

Wild Goose. Wild goose has a reputation for being tough, and often the reputation is deserved. However, the meat of young geese is delicious, nutritious, and juicy. Even an old, tough goose can be turned into tender, tasty fare by slow cooking. If you have a big one and suspect it may be tough, cut it into bite-size pieces, put it in a pot with whatever vegetables you like and chicken stock, and simmer it long and gently for a wonderful stew.

Thanksgiving Goose. Years ago it was customary in my family, as in many German families, to roast a goose for Thanksgiving. Here is how my mother did it. The necessary ingredients include: a large honker, snow, or blue goose, a quarter cup butter, a half cup uncooked rice, three sticks celery, one medium-size onion, two cups water, one and a half cups ground cranberries, two chicken bouillon cubes, one sprig parsley, one teaspoon salt, one teaspoon freshly ground pepper. Stuffing is made by melting butter in a skillet, adding rice, onion, and celery, and then cooking slowly while stirring constantly. When the rice is slightly brown and the cranberries and all the rest of the ingredients have been added, cover and cook slowly until the rice is tender. If the rice has a tendency to stick, add water. The stuffing is allowed to cool while the oven warms up to about 350 degrees. As soon as the stuffing is cool enough to handle, place it inside the goose,

and put the goose in a roaster, breast up. Basting it in its own juices, cook it for about four hours (for a six- to ten-pound bird).

OTHER GOOSE AND DUCK RECIPES

Another good way to cook a small goose is to use the recipe described before for ducks with sauerkraut. The meat of a wild goose can also be used in the duck Stroganoff recipe given before. Equally delicious is the filleted breast of a wild goose broiled over hickory charcoal. It may be necessary to cut the fillets from larger geese into thin strips before broiling. Use a liquor of wine vinegar, melted butter, and seasonings to baste the goose while it is being broiled.

Duck with Mushroom Gravy. One final waterfowl recipe that we have tried and enjoyed is one called duck with mushroom gravy, suggested by Joe Bates, author of *The Outdoor Cook's Bible*. For this, two ducks are needed, plus one sliced onion, a half cup butter or margarine, salt and pepper, one bay leaf, two cups water, one cup fresh sliced mushrooms, two tablespoons flour, and one-eighth teaspoon thyme. The ducks are disjointed into serving-size pieces. Brown the meat and the onion in fat until the onion is transparent and the duck a golden brown. Pour off the drippings into another skillet, season with salt and pepper, and add the water and bay leaf. Cover and cook over moderate heat for an hour and a half.

In a second skillet containing the drippings, sauté the sliced mushrooms and stir in the flour and thyme until the mixture is smooth. Add this to the ducks and continue to cook them slowly for about thirty minutes longer. Use one-half cup of wine instead of water, if desired. Serve with rice or barley.

Wild-Rice Casserole. To serve wild rice with wild duck is almost traditional in places, and here is a particularly elegant wild-rice casserole as prepared by Isabel Sayers. The ingredients include: one pound wild rice (cooked and drained), one pound mild sausage, one pound fresh mushrooms, one cup onions chopped, one-half cup toasted sliced almonds, one-fourth cup flour, one-half cup milk, two and one-half cups chicken bouillon, one table-spoon salt, one-half teaspoon pepper, a pinch of oregano, thyme, and marjoram, and an optional Tabasco dash or two. Sauté the sausage and drain enough fat from it to sauté the onions and mushrooms. Make a sauce of flour and milk, and add chicken bouillon. Simmer until thick. Add seasoning and other ingredients, pour into a casserole and top with almonds. Bake for thirty minutes in a 350-degree oven.

CHAPTER 13

THE FUTURE OF WATERFOWLING

Wildlife conservation is sometimes said to be in its infancy, and certainly that's true of wildlife *management* as a scientific discipline inextricably joined to large-scale land utilization. In America, this approach was first expounded in the early 1930s by Aldo Leopold, notably in his book *Game Management*. That same decade was marked by an unprecedented surge in governmental and private financing of conservation programs, some of which now benefit waterfowl more than ever and will continue to do so in the future.

During the late 1920s and early '30s a prolonged and very severe drought scourged much of North America. The Dust Bowl years brought starvation and misery to humanity and wild creatures alike. With the Great Depression deepening, funds were needed more desperately for soup kitchens than for conservation, which meant that our meager conservation agencies were inadequately financed and staffed. Yet the Roosevelt Administration sought innovative conservation schemes, partly because Frankin Delano Roosevelt was a sincere conservationist and partly for economic and political motives. Employment would be boosted by new public work programs involving land reclamation, refuge building and maintenance, and the like.

Conservation History

Thus, in 1934 Jay Norwood ("Ding") Darling, Roosevelt's newly appointed chief of the Biological Survey (forerunner of the Fish and Wild-

life Service), was able to recruit congressional support for a $1 federal waterfowling permit: the famous duck stamp. Originally designated the Migratory Bird Hunting Stamp, it is now officially called the Migratory Bird Hunting and Conservation Stamp, and at the time of this writing costs $10. Darling, a talented professional artist and political cartoonist, drew the

This is the first (1934–35) federal Migratory Bird Hunting Stamp—the famous "duck stamp," which is now designated as the Migratory Bird Hunting and Conservation Stamp. In the early days, it was validated by Post Office cancellation (postmark). Today the buyer must validate it by signing his name across its face, and in many parts of the country he must also buy and validate a state waterfowl stamp so that additional revenues can be accrued for wildlife conservation. The cost of the federal stamp has risen tenfold from the time it was initiated to the time of this writing.

design for the first (1934–35) stamp, depicting a hen and drake mallard alighting on the water. Since then, over 93 million duck stamps have been purchased. By 1987, the stamp sales had funneled more than $300 million into waterfowl conservation.

It was also in the mid-1930s that the first North American Wildlife Conference was convened—with enormous publicity thanks to Roosevelt's personal endorsement. Working with a broadbased coalition of conference delegates, Darling and several associates founded the National Wildlife Federation, which is now our largest and probably most powerful private, nonprofit conservation organization. In addition to raising vast sums for wildlife, NWF has become instrumental in forging conservation legislation and influencing America's conservation policies.

The first NWF triumph was the passage of the 1937 Pittman-Robertson Act (the Federal Aid in Wildlife Restoration Act) which levies excise taxes on sporting arms and ammunition, earmarking the funds for wildlife projects. In its first half century, this hunter-supported tax pro-

This is a clutch of black-duck eggs in an elevated nest box that was used during a breeding program and behavioral-modification experiment by the U.S. Fish & Wildlife Service at a famous research installation in Patuxent, Maryland. (*Luther Goldman, Bureau of Sport Fisheries & Wildlife*)

Although Canada's prairie-pothole provinces produce a majority of North America's waterfowl, a great many geese and ducks nest successfully in the upper United States. These Canada goslings were photographed in Wyoming. (*Wyoming Game & Fish Department*)

Here's what state and federal agencies and private, nonprofit conservation groups are striving for. These ducks—thousands of them—are utilizing the waters of a National Wildlife Refuge in North Dakota. (*North Dakota Game & Fish Department*)

gram has generated more than $1.5 billion for the conservation of waterfowl and all other wildlife.

Still another momentous event that affects waterfowling now and in the future was the founding of Ducks Unlimited, which was incorporated in Washington, D.C., in 1937. DU's parent organization, a small private foundation, had sponsored the first aerial survey, or census, of nesting waterfowl, in 1935, and Ducks Unlimited continued to pioneer new approaches to waterfowl management. By the early 1980s, DU had raised over $200 million for the benefit of waterfowl and had expanded its operations in habitat acquisition and improvement from Canada into parts of the United States and Mexico. By 1987, four million acres had been reserved by Du for wildlife, and the *annual* fundraising goal was $66.7 million.

Failure of Experimental Regulations

The achievements (as well as occasional disagreements) of private groups and the government will continue to have an impact on waterfowl populations. Unfortunately, so will

State and federal conservation personnel use aircraft for game and habitat surveys and for law enforcement. Here, Oklahoma Wildlife officers check an aerial map. (*Oklahoma Department of Wildlife Conservation*)

the mistakes, including a bag-limit system that must be reformed. When another prolonged drought in the 1950s caused a dwindling of waterfowl production, management was accelerated, seasons and bag limits curtailed, and in some years the season was closed on one or more species. Exceptional regulations for troubled species were hardly new, but beginning in 1961 there was a greatly sharpened emphasis on species management as opposed to general waterfowl management. Although some of the resulting experimentation still holds promise, some has failed.

One disappointment has been the "point system" to replace the simple bag limit of a given number of birds daily. This system theoretically allowed a total bag of 100 points, with different numbers assigned to birds of different species, and in some cases different point values for hens and drakes. Thus, a plentiful and relatively underharvested duck such as a bufflehead or shoveler (in one region or another) might cost only 10 points, while another species might cost 50. And a mallard drake might be worth only 20 points (on the theory that fewer surviving drakes are needed since one drake may breed with a number of hens) but a hen mallard might cost far more points. At present, between a quarter and a third of our states retain this system in some form (with the minimum point value doubled to 20), but it has been a controversial experiment, and it's probably safe to say that most waterfowl conservationists consider it a noble failure.

It has several glaring flaws. In some states, it simply allows hunters to kill more ducks per day than they should. It also depends heavily on in-flight waterfowl identification, which is difficult for many hunters. This makes game-law violators out of people who would be perfectly content to obey a simple limit on the number of birds bagged. It also provides an alibi for intentional cases of "mistaken identity." And it encourages the taking of "bonus ducks" and the practice of "reordering the bag." If a hunter has brought down 90 points' worth of ducks, he may remain in the blind to bag one more—and if that last duck turns out to be a 20-point drake mallard, the total will exceed 100 points, but a warden usually will follow the policy of allowing it. A bonus duck! On occasion, a gunner will bag a high-point duck first or second and go right on shooting, claiming afterward that the high-point duck was a bonus bird, killed last. This outrageous practice of reordering the bag cannot be excused in an age of reduced habitat and wildlife populations.

Many states have therefore reverted to the older, simpler system, and still other alternatives have been proposed. There is no question that for the sake of waterfowling's future we need reduced bag limits and seasons, at least for a few years—perhaps no more than three birds per day and no more than thirty (rather than fifty) days per year. During recent years of renewed drought, reduced habitat, increased numbers of hunters, and stabilized federal regulations, geese and swans have fared surprisingly well, as have some species of ducks—but others duck species have dwindled alarmingly, and their restoration must be implemented. James H. Phillips, a highly respected waterfowling journalist, recently suggested an innovative three/two/one formula for setting bag limits. His formula calls for a total limit of *three* ducks per day, including no more than *two* birds of any single species, and no more than *one* black duck, wood duck, canvasback (where cans are legal), hen mallard, or hen pintail.

In recent years we have seen a dwindling of these species and some others (notably bluewinged teal) that probably could have been avoided, at least in part. A major element in the difficulty emerged in 1979, when first Canada and then the United States announced a five-year plan for stabilized duck-hunting regulations. This experiment was to facilitate a long-term study of the effects of hunting pressure and other factors on duck populations, and the study would, in turn, facilitate a long-term North American management plan. Until then, season lengths and bag limits had fluctuated annually, based chiefly on breeding-ground censuses.

At the first indication of trouble, the stabilization experiment should have been abandoned. But the bureaucratic statisticians argued that cutting the program short would sacrifice the value of data already accumulated. Unfortunately, major sportsmen's conservation groups supported them, believing that the acquisition and improvement of sufficient habitat (that is, water) would be adequate to assure the multiplication of duck populations.

Since the early 1980s brought another prolonged drought—including three of the worst years since the Dust Bowl—there was less water rather than more, and nesting conditions were calamitous. When ducks don't have enough safe water on their nesting grounds, the problem of nesting failure is compounded by the proportionally increased success of predators and the subsequent increase in predator populations. And so summer mortality grew at the same time reproduction subsided. Because farmland potholes and sloughs were still being drained and tilled in the North, while wetlands in the South were being filled for residential, agricultural, and industrial development, both summer and winter habitat continued to shrink. And yet, during the first seven years of the 1980s, more than 120 million ducks were shot.

By 1985, however, the five-year stabilization period had ended, and not long afterward the Department of the Interior issued its inconclusive and rather ambiguous report on the study. A year later, states began to tighten their regulations and lower their bag limits. A rather embarrassing chapter in the history of waterfowl management was ended.

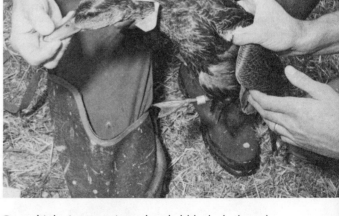

Game biologists examine a banded black duck at the Patuxent, Maryland, research facility. (*Luther Goldman, Bureau of Sport Fisheries & Wildlife*)

A biologist collects eggs from a nesting box at the Delta Marsh Waterfowl and Wetlands Research Station in Manitoba. (*Charles S. Potter, Jr.*)

A conservation officer collects live-trapped birds during a study project focusing on Mexican black ducks at Bosque del Apache National Wildlife Refuge in New Mexico. (*Luther Goldman, Bureau of Sport Fisheries & Wildlife*)

Governmental and Private Conservation and Research

I do not mean to imply that research and management programs have all been ill-advised or disappointing during the last few decades. For example, the wood duck is now a common duck rather than a rare one, even though it has been overharvested and is still threatened by a shortage of nesting habitat. Important strides have been made by state conservation agencies, the federal government, and many universities, often working together. An example often cited is the pioneering research of Dr. Frank C. Bellrose and his colleagues at the Illinois Natural History Survey. Those studies resulted in a vastly increased knowledge of waterfowl population dynamics, waterfowl diseases, the migrational behavior of mallards and black ducks, and many other aspects of waterfowl biology, behavior, and management. One of the studies was also instrumental in amassing evidence in support of nontoxic (steel) shot regulations to end the terrible waste of wildlife caused by lead poisoning. Comparably important research has been done at state and federal facilities in Maryland, Texas, Utah, California, and many other states.

A number of privately owned (or originally private) research installations have also aided significantly in waterfowl management. These include Remington Farms, originally owned by airplane manufacturer Glenn L. Martin and now owned by Remington Arms/DuPont; and Nilo Farms, owned by Winchester/Olin. One of the best-known and most productive is the Delta Marsh Waterfowl Research Station in Manitoba, originally a private duck hatchery owned by James Bell. In cooperation with the University of Wisconsin and Dr. Miles Pirnie, director of the W. K. Kellogg Bird Sanctuary, Bell transformed the hatchery into a research facility. For many years, the renowned Dr. Albert Hochbaum was director of the station, which eventually came to be administered by the privately endowed Wildlife Management Institute. Many modern waterfowl-management methods are derived from studies performed at the station. Incidentally, the Wildlife Management Institute also sponsored Frank C. Bellrose's 1976 revision of Francis H. Kortright's classic 1942 text

The Ducks, Geese and Swans of North America. In 1977 this revised edition was honored by the Wildlife Society as the year's outstanding publication in wildlife ecology and management.

During these same decades, outstanding work in waterfowl conservation and management has also continued under the auspices of previously mentioned nonprofit organizations, including Ducks Unlimited, the National Wildlife Federation, the National Audubon Society, and others. These organizations have, in addition, brought significant pressure to bear on state legislatures and the United States Congress. They have played a direct and crucial role in the writing and enactment of many important environmental laws during the 1960s, 1970s, and 1980s, and were also instrumental in the establishment of the Environmental Protection Agency. All of these groups are better funded than at any time in their history, and they can be expected to expand their wildlife programs. In addition, there is a foundation to which sportsmen can make donations with the stipulation that their money be used for waterfowl management. It's the National Fish and Wildlife Foundation (Room 2626, U.S. Department of the Interior, 18th and C Streets, Washington, D.C. 20240). Earmarked donations will be channeled directly into waterfowl projects staffed by U.S. and Canadian scientists.

North American Waterfowl Management Plan

One potentially positive result of the five-year U.S./Canadian stabilized-regulation study has been the formulation of a fifteen-year North American Waterfowl Management Plan, which specifies objectives for most species that would restore ducks to the population levels of the 1960s. This joint endeavor of the United States and Canada will involve not only further research projects but regulation adjustments and active management of habitat and wildlife. It is expected to cost $1.5 billion by the time it has fulfilled all of its objectives.

George Reiger, one of our most knowledgeable and perceptive conservation writers, believes it may take a decade or more to restore some of the duck species to the levels of the

The black duck, like the mallard, is a ground nester and will not readily accept elevated nesting boxes as wood ducks will. However, these black ducks were persuaded to lay their eggs in predator-proof elevated nests during a "behavioral-imprinting" study at the Patuxent, Maryland, research facility. (*Anthony J. Florio, U.S. Fish & Wildlife Service*)

An Oklahoma Wildlife Ranger checks the licenses and duck stamps of three waterfowlers. The Rangers and their counterparts in other states—as well as federal law-enforcement personnel—administer and enforce our game regulations. Cooperative sportsmen like these pay for the costs of enforcement, research, game management, and habitat enhancement.

1960s, and he has told me he never again expects to see the vast flocks he watched from his blind in the late 1940s and early 1950s. It's important to realize that today there are more than twice as many waterfowlers as there were in the 1930s when the duck stamp was introduced. And although we are not more skillful hunters than our predecessors, we are better equipped and the birds are concentrated on smaller tracts of migratory and wintering habitat. Hunting pressure will not be abated in terms of the number of gunners in the wetlands, nor is it likely to be abated by a diffusion of waterfowl over wider areas of habitat. Our struggle to conserve and increase habitat and to perfect wise waterfowl management techniques must continue.

But if we don't waver in that resolve, I believe we may have learned enough from previous setbacks to secure the future of waterfowling. The

In recent years a number of duck species—including the pintail, or sprig—have suffered an alarming decline in numbers. A major goal of the North American Waterfowl Management Plan, a joint undertaking of the United States and Canadian governments, is to restore them to levels of the 1960s. In this photo, you see a small portion of the hundreds of thousands of pintails that stop on their migration from far northern breeding grounds at the Sacramento National Wildlife Refuge near Willows, California. What we are striving for is to witness a great many more scenes like this. (*U.S. Fish & Wildlife Service*)

populations of Canada geese and tundra swans have surged because those species are so fertile, so resistant to adversity, and so adaptable to changing conditions. Snow geese, too, have exhibited a gratifying durability and adaptability. Among ducks, the mallard is a particular concern—a "target," you might say—of the North American Waterfowl Management Plan, and not just because it's our most widely distributed duck but because it's also the most fertile and adaptable. This may indicate that the bureaucratic planners and game biologists are hedging their bet, but it also indicates a strong promise of success. And in the process of succeeding with mallards, as well as with some of the other ducks and the geese, game managers are likely to gain the precious knowledge needed to keep the birds flying over our boats and blinds.

APPENDIX I

A GUIDE TO USING STEEL SHOT

Many of us gained our basic shotgunning skills while hunting upland birds and small game, and some of us honed those skills on clay targets. The pellets in our shells were lead, and the introduction of steel presented us with unfamiliar shooting problems. Even those hunters who have always specialized in waterfowling have, for the most part, gained more years of experience shooting lead than steel. There are important differences, and killing game cleanly and consistently requires an understanding of those differences.

Bob Brister, one of America's finest wingshots and foremost hunting writers, has pointed out that when hunters first start using steel, "there is usually a slight reduction in birds bagged. But once hunters become familiar with shooting steel, bags improve and in some instances have increased, probably due to a reduction in out-of-range shooting." Here are some guidelines that should help you use steel more efficiently.

Steel produces very tight patterns and a shot string that's shorter by about a third than a comparable string of lead pellets. Up to a point, a short shot string is desirable since it means that more of the pellets in the total load will reach a moving target in time to hit it. But an extremely short shot string combined with a tight pattern will require increased accuracy to avoid missing entirely or hitting with only a couple of pellets at the fringe of the pattern. Most of us can improve our accuracy (including our judgment of forward allowance on a flying target) by merely practicing, but we need all the help we can get. A large part of that help is just

a matter of using less choke in order to open up the shot pattern.

Full choke has been the traditional muzzle constriction for most waterfowling, but as a rule it's too tight for steel. It's even too tight for most modern lead-shot loads except for long-range pass-shooting. A tightly choked gun that delivers a 30-inch effective pattern at duck-decoying ranges when firing a high-velocity lead load may deliver only a 24-inch steel pattern at equal ranges. Thus the lead-shot pattern covers an area of 707 square inches while the steel covers only 452 square inches. That's a substantial reduction in hit probability, but it's easily remedied by using less choke.

It's no longer heresy to suggest using a modified rather than full choke for the majority of duck and goose shooting. It's just good sense. In fact, an even wider choke—improved cylinder—is apt to be best for teal and other fast, close-flying ducks. Bob Brister has found that an improved-modified choke (about .025 constriction) "produces the best patterns with the widest variety of loads and shot sizes," but he adds that "modified is a good all-around compromise."

Because steel is lighter than lead (hence, ballistically inferior), you need a larger steel pellet to retain energy equal to that of lead shot. Some manufacturers recommend going one size larger and others suggest going two sizes larger for a given shooting purpose. The seemingly contradictory recommendations really mean the same thing. The confusion arises because most brands of ammunition carry numerical designations that skip a number between some sizes.

In other words, No. 4 is one size larger than No. 6 because at present there's no No. 5 steel, and even No. 5 lead has become mighty hard to find in recent years. As a booklet published by Remington advises, "steel No. 4s would be used for situations where you previously used lead No. 6s."

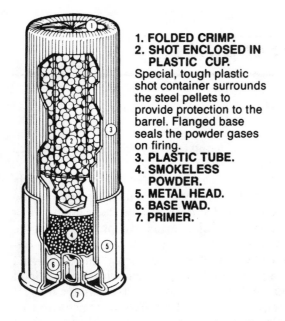

1. FOLDED CRIMP.
2. SHOT ENCLOSED IN
PLASTIC CUP.
Special, tough plastic shot container surrounds the steel pellets to provide protection to the barrel. Flanged base seals the powder gases on firing.
3. PLASTIC TUBE.
4. SMOKELESS
POWDER.
5. METAL HEAD.
6. BASE WAD.
7. PRIMER.

Construction and components of a Federal shotshell loaded with steel pellets. (*Courtesy of Federal Cartridge Company*)

Bear in mind, however, that the largest steel sizes are generally the tightest-patterning sizes, so under certain circumstances they can become too much of a good thing. If you use T or F shot, which are extremely large, you may be almost compelled to use an improved-cylinder choke because you'll probably get full-choke performance.

Pellet size must also be considered in terms of its effect on a gun's bore (and particularly on the choke). This applies both to screw-in choke tubes and to bores with a single integral choke. Some arms manufacturers will not warranty their shotguns against damage if steel sizes larger than BB are used. In addition, some will void a warranty if handloaded ammunition is used. (In the latter case, the reason is not pellet size but the fact that the manufacturer has no way of being certain that safe, properly loaded ammunition was fired through the gun.)

There is no denying that in factory-loaded shells, steel sizes as large as T and F have legitimate uses, but those uses are limited. F shot is intended for pass-shooting geese at the longest possible range, but many of us are convinced that few sportsmen (including ourselves) are skillful enough to bring down geese cleanly and consistently at more than 50 or perhaps 55 yards. The T size is a good bet for very large geese—for shooting in areas where the birds are likely to be greater Canadas, for instance. And it may offer an advantage in pass-shooting smaller geese, too, when there's a high wind, because it drifts less than the smaller sizes. (For the same reason, you might choose No. 1 steel for large ducks in a strong wind.) But ordinarily, most of us need nothing larger than No. 2 for the biggest ducks and nothing larger than BB for geese.

What about the "Duplex" factory loads that combine two sizes, such as "BB × 2" or "2 × 6"? In these shells, the heavier shot is loaded in front of the lighter shot. Regardless of such trade designations as "Multirange," the real purpose of this ammunition is not to lengthen effective range. The purpose is to combine a few large pellets, for deep game penetration, with a lot of smaller pellets, for more total energy in the pattern. The intention, then, is to increase the load's ability to kill game cleanly, with the same self-imposed limits on range that have always applied.

Regardless of shot size, there remains the question of whether steel pellets will damage a gun's bore. The answer depends on the gun—and on the choke tubes if the gun employs the interchangeable-tube system. Yes, steel shot may damage some older guns, and the danger is greatest to old double-barreled guns and guns with full choke. Even with some open-choked barrels, a ring bulge near the muzzle has been known to develop. Generally, this can be considered merely cosmetic damage since it's unlikely to have a significant effect on patterning. But cosmetic damage is a calamity when it happens to a treasured gun. An obvious general safeguard is simply not to use an old full-choked or double-barreled gun for waterfowling. But if you have any question about any gun, old or new, the safest course is to contact the manufacturer.

To aid you in the selection, test-patterning,

and use of steel-shot loads, here are some facts, tips, and tables supplied by ammunition manufacturers. From Federal Cartridge Company:

"Steel shot is made by forming soft steel wire into pellets, which are then annealed and coated. A steel pellet weighs about 30 percent less than a lead pellet of similar size. Therefore, there are more pellets in an ounce of steel shot than in an ounce of lead shot (of equal size). The size of shot, whether lead or steel, is based on American Standard shot sizes. Thus, a steel No. 4 pellet and a lead No. 4 pellet are both .130 inch in diameter."

Steel Shot Sizes:	6	4	3	2	1	BB	T	F
Shot Diameter (ins.)	.11	.13	.14	.15	.16	.18	.20	.22
Steel Pellets Per Ounce	315	192	158	125	103	72	52	40

Lead pellets per ounce: BB=50; 2=87; 4=135; 6=225

"Shotguns pattern differently when shooting steel, lead, or buffered lead loads. They also may perform differently when shooting pellets of different sizes in these types of loads. Hunters should experiment and pattern their shotguns at various distances with different shot sizes to get the optimum pattern densities regardless of what type of shell they are using."

Waterfowl Type	Suggested Pattern Density (# of pellets in a 30" circle at 40 yds.)
small ducks	140
medium ducks	110
large ducks	85
small geese	55
large geese	35

In the following comparison of led and steel pellet energy, also provided by Federal Cartridge Company, the muzzle velocity of the lead pellets is figured at 1,330 feet per second and the muzzle velocity of the steel pellets is figured at 1,365 feet per second.

Shot Type/Size	Pellet Energy in Foot/Pounds at Range (yards)			
	30	40	50	60
lead 7½	1.8			
steel 6	.9			
lead 6	3.0	2.3		
steel 4	3.5	2.5		
lead 4	5.6	4.4	3.4	
steel 2	6.0	4.4	3.4	
lead 2	9.5	7.5	6.1	4.9
steel BB	11.6	9.0	7.1	5.5
lead BB		15.0	12.0	10.0
steel T		20.0	18.0	16.0
steel F		24.0	22.0	20.0

The minimum energy required depends on the type of waterfowl being hunted and, as you can see in the table above, energy necessarily diminishes as range increases. At 30 yards, for example, steel No. 2 pellets have 6 foot/pounds of energy, but at 50 yards the figure drops to 3.4 foot/pounds. With these factors taken into account, Federal suggests the following steel sizes and shot weights:

STEEL SHOT GAME SELECTION GUIDE

Birds/Range	Recommended Steel Shot Sizes	Recommended Minimum Shot Wt.
Ducks under 35 yds.	2,3,4,6	¾ oz. +
Ducks 35-45 yds.	BB,1,2,3	1 oz. +
Ducks 45 yds. or more	BB,1,2	1⅛ oz.
Small Geese under 45 yds.	F,T,BB,1	1¼ oz.
Large Geese, any range/ Small Geese over 45 yds.	F,T,BBB,BB	1¼ oz.

Bear in mind that an ammunition company's recommendations are based on tests of that company's own loads, and may therefore vary slightly from recommendations of other manufacturers. For example, the accompanying chart of Remington's recommended steel loads does not include T, F, and BBB sizes but does include Duplex loads. Here are guidelines offered by Remington:

"Since individual pellet energy and total pattern energy increase directly and progressively for both lead and steel as pellet size increases, the largest pellet sizes would always seem to be better than smaller sizes. However, Remington's experience indicates that effective hunting at selected ranges depends on a balanced combination of both pellet energy (based on size) and pattern density. The steel loads recommended on the chart represent the best combination of steel pellet energy and pattern density to provide effective ballistic performance.''

Remington Recommended Steel Shot Loads*

Game Bird	Range Conditions**	Load	Gauge	Length In Inches	Oz. of Shot	Shot Size	Index Number
CANADA AND SNOW GEESE	Pass	Duplex™ Steel	12	3	1¼	BBX2	MRS12H
	Pass	Duplex™ Steel	12	2¾	1⅛	BBX2	MRS12
	Pass	Steel Magnum	12	3	1¼	BB,1	STL12MAG
	Pass	Steel Magnum	12	2¾	1¼	1	STL12SMAG
	Pass	Steel	12	2¾	1⅛	BB,1	STL12
	Over Decoys	Duplex™ Steel	12	3	1¼	BBX4	MRS12H
	Over Decoys	Steel Magnum	12	3	1¼	2	STL12MAG
	Over Decoys	Steel Magnum	12	2¾	1¼	2	STL12SMAG
	Over Decoys	Steel	12	2¾	1⅛	2	STL12
SMALLER GEESE Lesser Canadas, Blue, White-Fronted, Brant	Over Decoys	Duplex™ Steel	12	2¾	1⅛	BBX4	MRS12
	Over Decoys	Steel Magnum	12	3	1¼	4	STL12MAG
	Over Decoys	Steel Magnum	12	2¾	1¼	4	STL12SMAG
	Over Decoys	Steel	12	2¾	1⅛	4	STL12

NOTE: Effective steel loads include all those listed for Canada and Snow Geese plus loads of slightly smaller size listed above.

DUCKS	Pass & Decoys	Duplex™ Steel	12	3	1¼	BBX2	MRS12H
	Pass & Decoys	Duplex™ Steel	12	3	1¼	BBX4	MRS12H
	Pass & Decoys	Duplex™ Steel	12	2¾	1⅛	BBX2	MRS12
	Pass & Decoys	Steel Magnum	12	3	1¼	2,4	STL12MAG
	Pass & Decoys	Steel Magnum	12	2¾	1¼	2,4	STL12SMAG
	Pass & Decoys	Steel	12	2¾	1⅛	2	STL12
	Over Decoys	Duplex™ Steel	12	2¾	1⅛	BBX4	MRS12
	Over Decoys	Duplex™ Steel	12	2¾	1⅛	2X6	MRS12
	Over Decoys	Duplex™ Steel	12	3	1¼	2X6	MRS12H
	Over Decoys	Steel Magnum	12	3	1¼	6	STL12MAG
	Over Decoys	Steel	12	2¾	1⅛	4	STL12
	Over Decoys	Steel Magnum	20	3	1	2,4	STL20HMAG
SMALL WATERFOWL, TEAL, RAIL	Pass & Decoys	Duplex™ Steel	12	3	1¼	2X6	MRS12H
	Pass & Decoys	Duplex™ Steel	12	2¾	1⅛	2X6	MRS12
	Pass & Decoys	Steel Magnum	12	3	1¼	6	STL12MAG
	Pass & Decoys	Steel	12	2¾	1⅛	4,6	STL12
	Pass & Decoys	Steel Magnum	20	3	1	4,6	STL20HMAG

*Recommended loads. However, other Remington loads may be substituted based on individual preferences and experience.
**Pass Shooting—40 yards and over; Decoy Shooting—under 40 yards.

(Courtesy of Remington Arms)

APPENDIX II

HUNTER'S CHECKLIST OF NORTH AMERICAN WATERFOWL AND OTHER GAME BIRDS OF THE WETLANDS

NOTE: The following list includes normally hunted, wild native species. It does not include feral (originally domestic) birds such as the mute swan, which was long ago brought to America from Europe as a "park bird." It also omits Asian, European, and Latin American species which are rarely encountered in North America or encountered only in very restricted regions at the fringes of their range—for example, the Baikal Teal, European widgeon, and Mexican duck. And it omits numerous subspecies that can seldom be distinguished by laymen or that may be disputed by ornithologists— many geographic races of very similar Canada geese being a prime example. It also excludes hybrids, which are common but cannot be classified as species.

Following the common name of each bird in the list is its scientific name. These scientific (taxonomic) designations are frequently revised by the American Ornithological Union and by various other scientific institutions and organizations—with the result that they are almost constantly in dispute.

For example, you may have seen the snow goose listed in field guides and various reference works (particularly older ones) as *Chen caerulescens*, but in some of the newer references it's listed as *Anser caerulescens*—a more accurate taxonomic designation. For the nomenclature given below, I have relied on a source considered to be exceptionally authoritative by wildlife-management agencies: *Ducks, Geese & Swans of North America*, by Frank C. Bellrose (Third Revised Edition, Stackpole, 1980). In most but not all instances, Bellrose is in agreement with the AOU and recent publications of the National Audubon Society. His designations are based on current taxonomic studies.

Swans

Trumpeter Swan—*Cygnus buccinator*
Whistling, or Tundra, Swan—*Cygnus columbianus*

Geese

American, or Atlantic, Brant—*Branta bernicla hrota*
Black Brant—*Branta bernicla nigricans*
Cackling Goose—*Branta canadensis minima*
Canada Goose—*Branta canadensis*
(Ten generally accepted Canada subspecies in addition to the Cackling Goose)
Emperor Goose—*Anser canagicas*
Hawaiian Goose, or Nene—*Branta sandvicensis*
Ross's Goose—*Anser rossi*
Greater Snow Goose—*Anser caerulescens atlantica*

Lesser Snow Goose—*Anser caerulescens caeru-lescens*

Blue Goose: now classified as color phase of the Lesser Snow; same scientific name

Tule Goose—*Anser albifrons gambelli*

White-fronted Goose—*Anser albifrons frontalis*

Ducks

Baldpate, or American Widgeon—*Anas americana*

Black Duck—*Anas rubripes*; also classified as *A. platyrhynchos rubripes*

Bufflehead—*Bucephala albeola*

Canvasback—*Aythya valisineria*

American, or Common, Eider—*Somateria mollissima*

King Eider—*Somateria spectabilis*

Gadwall—*Anas strepera*

Harlequin Duck—*Histrionicus histrionicus*

American, or Common, Goldeneye—*Bucephala clangula americana*

Barrow's Goldeneye—*Bucephala islandica*

Mallard—*Anas platyrhynchos platyrhynchos*

American, or Common, Merganser—*Mergus merganser americanus*

Hooded Merganser—*Mergus cucullatus*

Red-breasted Merganser—*Mergus serrator*

Old Squaw—*Clangula hyemalis*

Pintail, or Sprig—*Anas acuta acuta*

Redhead—*Aythya americana*

Ringneck Duck—*Aythya collaris*

Ruddy Duck—*Oxyura jamaicensis rubida*

Greater Scaup—*Aythya marila mariloides*

Lesser Scaup—*Aythya affinis*

American, or Black, Scoter—*Melanitta nigra americana*

Surf Scoter—*Melanitta perspicillata*

Whitewing Scoter—*Melanitta fusca deglandi*

Shoveler, or Northern Shoveler—*Anas clypeata*

Bluewing Teal—*Anas discors*

Cinnamon Teal—*Anas cyanoptera septentrionalium*

Greenwing Teal—*Anas crecca carolinensis*

Black-bellied Tree, or Whistling, Duck—*Dendrocygna autumnalis autumnalis*

Fulvous Tree, or Whistling, Duck—*Dendrocygna bicolor helva*

Wood duck—*Aix sponsa*

Shore and Marsh Birds

American, or common, coot—*Fulica americana*

Lesser Sandhill Crane—*Grus canadensis canadensis*

Common, or Florida, Gallinule—*Gallinula chloropus*

Clapper Rail—*Rallus longirostris*

King Rail—*Rallus elegans*

Sora Rail—*Porzana carolina*

Virginia Rail—*Rallus limicola*

Common, or Wilson's, Snipe, or Jacksnipe—*Capella gallinago*

APPENDIX III

UNITED STATES AND CANADIAN (STATE, PROVINCIAL, AND TERRITORIAL) WILDLIFE REGULATORY AGENCIES

States

ALABAMA:
Alabama Department of Conservation & Natural Resources
64 N. Union St.
Montgomery, AL 36130

ALASKA:
Alaska Department of Fish & Game
P.O. Box 3-2000
Juneau, AK 99802

ARIZONA:
Arizona Game & Fish Department
2222 W. Greenway Rd.
Phoenix, AZ 85023

ARKANSAS:
Arkansas Game & Fish Commission
#2 Natural Resources Dr.
Little Rock, AR 72205

CALIFORNIA:
California Department of Fish & Game
1416 Ninth St.
Sacramento, CA 95814

COLORADO:
Colorado Division of Wildlife
6060 Broadway
Denver, CO 80216

CONNECTICUT:
Connecticut Wildlife Bureau
Room 252, State Office Bldg.
165 Capitol Ave.
Hartford, CT 06106

DELAWARE:
Delaware Division of Fish & Wildlife
89 Kings Hwy., Box 1401
Dover, DE 19903

FLORIDA:
Florida Game & Fresh Water Fish Commission
620 S. Meridian St.
Tallahassee, FL 32301

GEORGIA:
Georgia Department of Natural Resources
Floyd Towers East
205 Butler St., S.E.
Atlanta, GA 30334

HAWAII:
Division of Forestry & Wildlife
Hawaii Department of Land & Natural
　Resources
1151 Punchbowl St.
Honolulu, HI 96813

IDAHO:
Idaho Fish & Game Department
600 S. Walnut, Box 25
Boise, ID 83707

ILLINOIS:
Permit Office
Illinois Department of Conservation
Lincoln Tower Plaza, 524 S. Second St.
Springfield, IL 62706

INDIANA:
Indiana Division of Fish & Wildlife
607 State Office Bldg.
Indianapolis, IN 46204

IOWA:
Iowa Conservation Commission
Wallace State Office Bldg.
Des Moines, IA 50319

KANSAS:
Kansas Fish & Game Commission
R.R. 2, Box 54A
Pratt, KS 67124

KENTUCKY:
Kentucky Department of Fish & Wildlife
　Resources
#1 Game Farm Rd.
Frankfort, KY 40601

LOUISIANA:
Louisiana Wildlife & Fisheries Commission
Box 15570
Baton Rouge, LA 70895

MAINE:
Maine Department of Inland Fisheries &
　Wildlife
284 State St., Station 41
Augusta, ME 04333

MARYLAND:
Wildlife Administration
Maryland Department of Natural Resources
Tawes State Office Bldg.
Annapolis, MD 21401

MASSACHUSETTS:
Massachusetts Fish & Wildlife Headquarters
Westboro, MA 01581

MICHIGAN:
Michigan Department of Natural Resources
Box 30028
Lansing, MI 48909

MINNESOTA:
Division of Fish & Wildlife
Minnesota Department of Natural Resources
500 Lafayette Rd.
St. Paul, MN 55146

MISSISSIPPI:
Mississippi Department of Wildlife
　Conservation
Box 451
Jackson, MS 39205

MISSOURI:
Missouri Department of Conservation
Box 180
Jefferson City, MO 65102

MONTANA:
Montana Department of Fish, Wildlife & Parks
1420 E. Sixth
Helena, MT 59620

NEBRASKA:
Nebraska Game & Parks Commission
Box 30370
Lincoln, NE 68503

NEVADA:
Nevada Department of Wildlife
Box 10678
Reno, NV 89520

NEW HAMPSHIRE:
New Hampshire Fish & Game Department
34 Bridge St.
Concord, NH 03301

NEW JERSEY:
New Jersey Division of Fish, Game & Wildlife
CN 400
Trenton, NJ 08625

NEW MEXICO:
New Mexico Game & Fish Department
Villagra Bldg.
Santa Fe, NM 87503

NEW YORK:
Bureau of Wildlife
New York Department of Environmental
   Conservation
50 Wolf Rd.
Albany, NY 12233

NORTH CAROLINA:
North Carolina Wildlife Resources Commission
512 N. Salisbury St.
Raleigh, NC 27611

NORTH DAKOTA:
North Dakota Game & Fish Department
100 N. Bismarck Expressway
Bismarck, ND 58501

OHIO:
Ohio Division of Wildlife
1500 Dublin Rd.
Columbus, OH 43215

OKLAHOMA:
Oklahoma Department of Wildlife Conservation
Box 53465
Oklahoma City, OK 73152

OREGON:
Oregon Department of Fish & Wildlife
Box 59
Portland, OR 97207

PENNSYLVANIA:
Pennsylvania Game Commission
Box 1567
Harrisburg, PA 17105

RHODE ISLAND:
Rhode Island Division of Fish & Wildlife
Tower Hill Rd., Washington County Govern-
   ment Center
Wakefield, RI 02879

SOUTH CAROLINA:
South Carolina Wildlife Resources Department
Box 167
Columbia, SC 29202

SOUTH DAKOTA:
South Dakota Game, Fish & Parks Department
445 E. Capitol
Pierre, SD 57501

TENNESSEE:
Tennessee Wildlife Resources Agency
Box 40747
Nashville, TN 37204

TEXAS:
Texas Parks & Wildlife Department
4200 Smith School Rd.
Austin, TX 78744

UTAH:
Utah Division of Wildlife Resources
1596 W. North Temple
Salt Lake City, UT 84116

VERMONT:
Vermont Fish & Wildlife Department
Montpelier, VT 05602

VIRGINIA:
Virginia Commission of Game & Inland
   Fisheries
Box 11104
Richmond, VA 23230

WASHINGTON:
Washington Department of Game
600 N. Capitol Way
Olympia, WA 98504

WEST VIRGINIA:
West Virginia Division of Wildlife
1800 Washington St., E.
Charleston, WV 24305

WISCONSIN:
Wisconsin Department of Natural Resources
Box 7921
Madison, WI 53707

WYOMING:
Wyoming Game & Fish Department
Cheyenne, WY 82002

Canadian Provinces

ALBERTA:
Alberta Fish & Wildlife Division
Main Floor, North Tower
Petroleum Plaza, 9945 108 St.
Edmonton, Alberta, Canada T5K 2C9

BRITISH COLUMBIA:
Wildlife Management Branch
British Columbia Ministry of Environment
Parliament Bldg.
Victoria, British Columbia, Canada V8V 1X5

MANITOBA:
Wildlife Branch
Manitoba Department of Natural Resources
Box 22, 1495 St. James St.
Winnipeg, Manitoba, Canada R3H 0W9

NEW BRUNSWICK:
Fish & Wildlife Branch
New Brunswick Department of Natural
    Resources
Box 6000
Fredericton, New Brunswick, Canada E3B 5H1

NEWFOUNDLAND/LABRADOR:
Wildlife Division
Newfoundland Department of Culture,
    Recreation & Youth
Bldg. 810, Box 4750
St. John's, Newfoundland, Canada A1C 5T7

NOVA SCOTIA:
Nova Scotia Department of Lands & Forests
Box 698
Halifax, Nova Scotia, Canada B3J 2T9

ONTARIO:
Wildlife Inquiries
Ontario Ministry of Natural Resources
Parliament Bldg.
Toronto, Ontario, Canada M7A 1W3

PRINCE EDWARD ISLAND:
Fish & Wildlife Division
Prince Edward Island Department of
    Community & Cultural Affairs
P.O. Box 2000
Charlottetown, Prince Edward Island,
    Canada C1A 7N8

QUEBEC:
Quebec Department of Recreation, Fish & Game
Place de la Capitale
150 E. St. Cyrille Blvd.
Quebec City, Quebec, Canada G1R 4Y1

SASKATCHEWAN:
Saskatchewan Department of Tourism &
    Renewable Resources
3211 Albert St.
Regina, Saskatchewan, Canada S4S 5W6

Canadian Territories

NORTHWEST TERRITORIES:
Wildlife Service
N.W.T. Department of Renewable Resources
Yellowknife, Northwest Territories,
Canada X1A 2L9

YUKON TERRITORY:
Wildlife & Parks Services
Yukon Department of Renewable Resources
Box 2703
Whitehorse, Yukon Territory,
Canada Y1A 2C6

About the Authors

ERWIN BAUER is a full-time outdoor writer and photographer whose articles have appeared in many magazines, including *Sports Illustrated, Outdoor Life, National Geographic,* and *Audubon.* With his wife, Peggy, he has written numerous books on outdoor sports and nature, including *The Bass Fisherman's Bible* and *The Saltwater Fisherman's Bible,* also in this series. The Bauers live in Jackson Hole, Wyoming.

ROBERT ELMAN is a writer and editor who specializes in subjects related to outdoor recreation, conservation, and nature study. His hunting and fishing articles have appeared in *Field & Stream, Sports Afield, Outdoor Life, The American Hunter, Gray's Sporting Journal,* and many other magazines. He has also written a score of books—most of them on outdoor sports—and some of his works have been translated into seven languages for publication abroad. With his wife, Ellen (a concert oboist), and their two young children, he lives on the remnant of an almost-two-hundred-year-old farm in rural New Jersey.

Bestselling guides to the great outdoors

THE OUTDOOR BIBLES

Written by top-notch field, stream and wilderness experts, this classic illustrated series on outdoor sports is ideal for novices and experts alike.

15155-1	**The Archer's Bible** by Fred Bear	$7.95
14993-X	**The Bass Fisherman's Bible** by Erwin A. Bauer	$7.95
17050-5	**The Camper's Bible (Rev. Ed.)** by Bill Riviere	$7.95
07276-7	**The Canoer's Bible** by Robert Douglas Mead	$7.95
14075-4	**The Climber's Bible** by Robin Shaw	$7.95
19985-6	**The Deer Hunter's Bible** by George Laycock	$7.95
14405-9	**The Fresh-Water Fisherman's Bible** by Vlad Evanoff	$7.95
24102-X	**The Golfer's Bible (Rev. Ed.)** by Frank Kenyon Allen, Tom LoPresti, Dale Mead, Barbara Romack	$7.95
18291-0	**The Gunner's Bible** by Bill Riviere and Robert Elman	$7.95
18343-7	**The Horseman's Bible** by Jack Coggins	$7.95
17219-2	**The Hunter's Bible** by W. K. Merrill and Clair Rees	$7.95
23747-2	**The Rifleman's Bible** by Sam Fadala	$7.95
18874-9	**The Runner's Bible** by Marc Bloom	$7.95
17220-6	**The Salt Fisherman's Bible** by Erwin A. Bauer	$7.95
23907-6	**The Shotgunner's Bible** by George Laycock	$7.95
13543-2	**The Skin Diver's Bible** by Owen Lee	$7.95
13057-0	**The Stargazer's Bible** by William S. Kals	$7.95
14406-7	**The Trout Fisherman's Bible** by Dan Holland	$7.95
24474-6	**The Waterfowler's Bible (Rev. Ed.)** by Erwin A. Bauer and Robert Elman	$7.95

At your local bookstore or for credit card orders of $25.00 or more, call toll free 1-800-223-6834, ext. 9479. In New York, Alaska and Hawaii, please call1-212-492-9479 and have your credit card handy. Or send your order, plus $2.00 for shipping and handling to the address below. (Please send checks or money orders only, no cash or C.O.D.'s).

DOUBLEDAY READERS SERVICES DEPT. OB2
P.O. BOX 5071, DES PLAINES, IL. 60017-5071

Prices and availability are subject to change without notice. Please allow four to six weeks for delivery.

A division of Bantam Doubleday Dell Publishing Group, Inc.